The Slave Trade
in Africa

An Ongoing Holocaust

Simon Webb

PEN & SWORD HISTORY

AN IMPRINT OF PEN & SWORD BOOKS LTD.
YORKSHIRE – PHILADELPHIA

First published in Great Britain in 2023 by
Pen & Sword History
An imprint of
Pen & Sword Books Ltd
Yorkshire - Philadelphia

ISBN 978 1 39909 407 8

A CIP catalogue record for this book is available from the British Library

Typeset in INDIA by IMPEC eSolutions
Printed and bound in the UK by CPI Group (UK) Ltd, Croydon, CRO 4YY

Pen & Sword Books Limited incorporates the imprints of Atlas, Archaeology, Aviation, Discovery, Family History, Fiction, History, Maritime, Military, Military Classics, Politics, Select, Transport, True Crime, Air World, Frontline Publishing, Leo Cooper, Remember When, Seaforth Publishing, The Praetorian Press, Wharncliffe Local History, Wharncliffe Transport, Wharncliffe True Crime and White Owl.

For a complete list of Pen & Sword titles please contact
PEN & SWORD BOOKS LIMITED
47 Church Street, Barnsley, South Yorkshire S70 2AS, United Kingdom
E-mail: enquiries@pen-and-sword.co.uk
Website: www.pen-and-sword.co.uk

or

PEN AND SWORD BOOKS
1950 Lawrence Rd, Havertown, PA 19083, USA
E-mail: Uspen-and-sword@casematepublishers.com
Website: www.penandswordbooks.com

Contents

List of Illustrations

Introduction

In recent decades, something very odd has happened to discussions and writing about slavery and the trade in slaves. From being considered as a general practice, something seen across the entire world throughout the whole of recorded history, as was once the case, the phrase 'slave trade' is now almost invariably preceded by a definite article; as in *the* slave trade. This is immediately understood by readers and listeners to refer to the transatlantic slave trade, in which black Africans were transported across the Atlantic Ocean from West Africa to the Americas. Despite the fact that this was by no means the only, or even the most extensive or cruel, trafficking in slaves which the world has seen, this particular type of slavery has become the only slave trade of which many people have even heard. If we see a book called *The Slave Trade*, we can be sure that the focus will be upon the horrors of the so-called Middle Passage and that any other type of slavery is hardly likely to get a look-in.

Here are one or two examples of the kind of book about slavery which is typically to be found in libraries and schools. *The Slave Trade* is by Tom Monaghan. It was published by Evans Brothers Ltd in 2002. A single side of one page deals with the 4,000-year recorded history of slavery and the trade in slaves. Apart from two pages at the end of the book, dealing with the modern slave trade, the rest of the book is concerned only with the transatlantic slave trade. Another book with the same title was written by Nigel Sadler and issued by Shire Publications in 2009. It too deals exclusively with the transatlantic slave trade. One more book called *The Slave Trade* should be sufficient to make the point. This one is by James Walvin and was published in

2011 by Thames & Hudson. Like the other two, it treats only of the transatlantic slave trade.

All this is very curious. The first written mention of slavery dates back as far as 2,000 BC and from that time up until the present day, slavery of one kind and another has been seen across the world. Until relatively lately, nobody in Britain would have dreamed of referring to the traffic from West Africa to the Americas and Caribbean as *the* slave trade. After all, Britain had its own experience of slavery to dwell on. Every schoolchild knew about Caractacus being taken in chains to Rome after the country was occupied by Roman forces, the fierce struggle of Boudicca to throw off the yoke of Roman tyranny and of course that seminal story of how the English first acquired their national identity; the anecdote related by the Venerable Bede about an incident in a slave market in Rome.

The Venerable Bede was an ecclesiastical historian working in Britain during the Anglo-Saxon period. He told the story of Pope Gregory who, in the sixth century AD, passed by a slave market in Rome. Seeing some beautiful, fair-haired children for sale, he enquired as to their origin and was told that they were 'Angli' or Angles, whereupon he made a pun in Latin. Gregory said, 'Non Angli sed Angeli'; not Angles but angels. It was after telling this story that Bede began referring to those living in the south-east part of Britain as English. Slavery was, until a few decades ago, known by every English person as something which their ancestors were likely to have endured. Pope Gregory and the English slaves may be seen in Illustration 1.

With the increasing emphasis on the transatlantic slave trade in both school history lessons and generally when the subject of slavery is mentioned, this early history of slavery involving English people has faded from memory. The decline in regular church attendance has led also to a reduced familiarity with Bible stories, a number of which also mention slavery. The story of Joseph, favourite son of Jacob and Rachel in the Book of Genesis, who was sold into slavery by his brothers, is probably the only such story of which most people today have heard. Knowledge of these different kinds of slavery, in Europe and the Middle East, is now restricted to those with a special and particular interest in history, rather than being the kind of thing which is picked up in the course of an ordinary childhood. It is perhaps inevitable that the subjects covered in school history lessons should, over the years, change and the increasing prominence given to slavery in North America and the Caribbean simply indicates that it is more relevant to many young people in Britain today than incidents from sixth-century Rome. There is nothing sinister in the fact that the history taught to children today is different from that which featured in lessons 60 or 70 years ago. One aspect of slavery though is quite deliberately hidden and we avoid talking of it from a misplaced sense of delicacy. This is the undeniable fact that the continent where slavery now flourishes as never before is also the one where it has always been a very popular activity as far back as we can look. Nobody wishes to be reminded about slavery in Africa. That white people took black slaves away from Africa is fine to talk about, but few want to be told that those slaves were sold to the white men by black African slave traders and that the ownership and sale of slaves in Africa was a vital part of the transatlantic trade.

So unpalatable is the notion of black involvement in slavery and the slave trade in Africa felt to be, that modern books do their best to brush the subject under the carpet whenever possible. Looking at an example of the way in which this is done might be informative. Here is a popular book on history which was published two years before the millennium. Called *The Mammoth Book of How it Happened*, it contains 200 eyewitness accounts of historical events, from life in ancient Sumer to the death of Princess Diana in 1997. The passage at which we are about to look is headed, 'Captured by slave traders, Eastern Nigeria 1756'. This extract is from the autobiography of Olaudah Equiano, a former slave who was born and spent his boyhood in the Igbo-speaking part of what is today Nigeria: 'My father . . . had a numerous family, of which seven lived to grow up, including myself and sister, who was the only daughter' (Lewis, 1998). The ellipsis, those three dots which indicate that some words have been omitted, is curious. This section of the book consists of two closely printed sides, perhaps a thousand words. Could it be that there was a long and irrelevant section which has been left out to economise on space? Well, no. Just three words have been removed. There was plenty of room for them. How did that sentence run in the original document? Here it is: 'My father, besides many slaves, had a numerous family, of which seven lived to grow up, including myself and a sister, who was the only daughter' (Equiano, 1789).

Right there, we see the nature of the problem and the reason that it was felt better to leave out those three words. The revelation that Olaudah Equiano's father, a black African living in Africa, owned many slaves is felt to be a little much for modern sensibilities. The idea that an African man might be buying, selling and owning slaves is, for many people, a shocking and distasteful thing.

Later in the extract from Equiano's book, another ellipsis is used. He describes how he and his sister were kidnapped by slave traders when their parents had left them at home one day. They were bound and gagged and carried far from their own village. We read a heart-rending and affecting account of Equiano and his sister being separated by the slave traders who have seized them and sold to different people; 'The next day proved a day of greater sorrow that I had yet experienced; for my sister and I were then separated, while we lay clasped in each other's arms.'

Let us see how the conclusion of this sad incident is set out in the modern book.

> I cried and grieved continually; and for several days did not eat anything but what they forced into my mouth . . .
> I was soon put down under the decks, and there I received such a salutation in my nostrils as I had never experience in my life (Lewis, 1998).

This all seems pretty clear to anybody reading these words today. A black slave has been parted from his sister and he has now been thrust below the decks of a ship. This fits in perfectly with our knowledge of the transatlantic slave trade. What more needs to be said?

It is time to explain what is going on here. The slave traders who seized Olaudah Equiano and his sister were themselves black Africans and their kidnapping had nothing at all to do with the transatlantic slave trade. This was simply the way of life in Africa, as it had been for as long as anybody could remember. White people and their ships were not part of this. Just as Equiano's father had many slaves, so too did other wealthy people in Africa. The men who took Equiano and his sister from their home did not sell them to white slave traders but to another Igbo family. That second ellipsis conceals a story of life as a black slave, owned by black people in Africa. That this was the state of affairs at that time, and a way of life which predated any European involvement in that part of the world, has not only been all but forgotten but is deliberately concealed from view, as we saw in the extracts above.

The book described above is no isolated example of the way in which people avoid mentioning slavery as practised in Africa. The British Library in London has a copy of the second edition of *The Interesting Narrative of the Life of Olaudah Equiano or Gustavus Vassa, the African* and this is what they have to say about it on their website, which was accessed in the summer of 2021.

> Equiano was born in what is now Nigeria and sold into slavery aged 11. After spells in Barbados and Virginia he spent eight years travelling the world as slave to a British Royal Navy officer, who renamed him Gustavus Vassa (British Library, 2021).

Once again, the impression is carefully created that Equiano had been captured as part of the transatlantic slave trade.

Although the transatlantic slave trade is so widely discussed, taught in schools and generally focused upon when the topic of slavery comes up, there appears to be some sort of mental block which prevents those who write about or talk of this particular trade from addressing the way in which it actually operated and how it was sustained. One sometimes gains the impression that the average person has the strange notion that the whole business ran smoothly with white Europeans controlling every aspect and black Africans featuring in the narrative just as helpless victims. A moment's thought will soon show the absurdity of this idea. Perhaps readers would like to pause at this point and ask themselves a simple question. A ship with a crew of perhaps fifty men anchors off the coast of West Africa. How did that small company go about loading up their ship with hundreds of slaves to take across the Atlantic Ocean?

Despite a general and widespread awareness of the transatlantic slave trade, an awful lot of people give little or no thought to the mechanics of the business. Did the crew go ashore and start rounding up people at gunpoint? This would have been a hazardous enterprise and one which would probably need more than a few dozen men. The ships would typically carry anything from between 250 to 600 slaves. Outnumbered ten to one, the logistics of such a hunting expedition would create all manner of problems. Were there perhaps British soldiers present to help with the roundup? In fact, most of the traffic took place in independent African kingdoms. What would the African warriors be doing while the white men were capturing their people; just standing idly by? It is only when we remember that the slave trade across the Atlantic was part of what is often called the 'Triangular Trade' that things begin to make sense.

The Triangular Trade began in Liverpool or Bristol, when ships would be loaded with manufactured goods such as muskets, gunpowder, brass, iron bars, glass beads, mirrors and various other things. These were items which were unobtainable in West Africa, unless they were acquired from European traders. The ships then set sail for Africa.

The cargoes of manufactured goods were a vital part of the Triangular Trade, because on arrival at their destination they would be traded for slaves. The slaves had already been rounded up by African slave dealers. They were, in the main, captives who had been seized from other tribes. Once loaded onto ships, the slaves were taken across the Atlantic to North America, South America or the Caribbean. The proceeds from their sale were then taken back across the sea to Britain, in the form of cotton, sugar and other produce, such as tobacco, for which there was a demand. Once the ships had returned to Liverpool and Bristol, the produce would be traded and exchanged for more manufactured goods and the cycle would begin again.

This then is the aspect of the transatlantic slave trade which is skirted around or preferably ignored altogether; that without the cooperation and cupidity of black African slave traders, there would not have been any slaves in the Caribbean or the southern states of America. The system relied upon the simple fact that slavery, and the buying and selling of slaves, was an old African tradition which had been around long before the ships containing white Europeans had ever appeared off the African coast. The slaves taken across the Atlantic were all bought and paid for. The white traders had no need to use violence or coercion to get hold of them, it was simply a business transaction between two sets of slave traders; one of which consisted of white Europeans and the other of black Africans. Illustration 2 is of black slave traders with their captives.

The modern reluctance to face an uncomfortable fact, that this slave trade was no more than an extension of one in which Africans had engaged since time immemorial, is a recent phenomenon. Sixty years ago, none of this would have been considered surprising and even children's books referred quite casually to the existence of black African slave traders. In 1960 a book about the life of the missionary David Livingstone was published by the British publisher Ladybird. 'Ladybird Books' of this kind, as older readers will know them, were commonly found in libraries and schools and many families had a few at home as well. They formed a background to childhood, at least in Britain, during the 1960s. Here, we read that:

> What was known as 'the slave trade' was being carried on all over this part of Africa. Men, women and children were captured by fierce savages, and then sold as slaves. Livingstone determined to do what he could to stop this terrible state of things (Peach, 1960).

On the next page, the following may be found:

> The savage slave traders were not long in trying to revenge themselves on Livingstone for having freed the slaves. One day, when he was travelling with a party of missionaries who had come out from England, they were suddenly attacked by the Ajawas (Peach, 1960).

The extracts above from a popular children's book were accompanied by colourful and vivid illustrations which showed quite clearly that the slave traders whom David Livingstone had so angered were all black. Even the tribe to which they belonged is named. In other words, 60 years ago the phrase 'the slave trade', which is used in the text of the book, had no connotations about white slavers or the transatlantic slave trade. It was simply a neutral way of referring to the seizing, buying and selling of human beings as though they were cattle and could just as easily have referred to ancient Rome, black Africa or the Arab nations of the Middle East.

The purpose of this chapter is really to dispel a common myth about Africa. Although few people ever put the matter into words or follow their ideas to a logical conclusion, an awful lot of white people in Europe and America hold views about pre-colonial Africa which owe a good deal to the eighteenth-century concept of the 'noble savage'.

There was in the seventeenth and eighteenth centuries a tendency to romanticize those from cultures other than that of Europe. This was done with native Americans and Africans in particular. The idea was that people who lived in unsophisticated and primitive societies were in some vague sense more 'natural' and that they were free of the vices which were thought to be a product of civilization at that time. Greed and envy, for instance, were considered to be caused by modern life and it was thought that in an African or native American village, everybody would share what they had and nobody would be rich or poor. Such people were believed by some to be more in tune with the natural world and more virtuous than those who lived in great cities and were constantly trying to exploit others and become wealthy. This led to the idea of the 'noble savage', untainted by all the bad aspects of modern civilization.

Alexander Pope wrote a poem in the early eighteenth century which summed up the distorted view about the difference between 'savages' and those who lived in civilized lands.

> Lo, the poor Indian! whose untutor'd mind
> Sees God in clouds, or hears him in the wind;
> His soul proud Science never taught to stray
> Far as the solar walk or milky way;
> Yet simple nature to his hope has giv'n,
> Behind the cloud-topt hill, an humbler Heav'n,
> Some safer world in depth of woods embraced,
> Some happier island in the wat'ry waste,
> Where slaves once more their native land behold,
> No fiends torment, no Christians thirst for gold.
> To be, contents his natural desire;
> He asks no Angel's wing, no Seraph's fire;
> But thinks, admitted to that equal sky,
> His faithful dog shall bear him company.

It is a pleasing vision of a simple man who is more in touch with nature, and God, than white Europeans. He has no 'thirst for gold' and is happy simply 'to be'.

This mentality is still going strong today. Many people in the West believe that the native inhabitants of both North and South America lived a peaceful life, attuned with the natural world and that they respected the land in the style of a modern climate-change activist. Hand in hand with such ideas goes the traditional view of the noble savage, that before the coming of Europeans to Africa or the Americas life was simpler and free of many of the less desirable character traits which we see in industrialized countries. These were people free of the mad obsession with acquiring consumer goods or piling up money in banks. Their lives were uncomplicated and gentler than those of us involved in the modern world and we could learn from examining such people and perhaps adopting their philosophical outlook on life. If only we too could attain such a state of being so that, as Pope put it:

> No fiends torment, no Christians thirst for gold.
> To be, contents his natural desire;
> He asks no Angel's wing, no Seraph's fire;
> But thinks, admitted to that equal sky,
> His faithful dog shall bear him company.

This fantasy touches upon our flawed perception of slavery and the slave trade. Captivated as we are by the thought of the pastoral and thoroughly natural life led by all those folk in Africa before the wicked Europeans came along and spoiled it all, we cannot quite bring ourselves to believe that some black Africans were every bit as keen on keeping, buying and selling black slaves as any of those men whose statues have been pulled down in Britain and the United States. Better by far to pile all the blame for such a detestable trade on the avarice and greed of British and American businessmen.

A marvellous instance of this attitude appeared on the Internet at the time of writing, in the autumn of 2021. On 21 September 2021, Professor Brittney Cooper of Rutgers University debated Critical Race Theory with a man called Michael Harriot. Both Cooper and Harriot are African-Americans and their conversation was published on a YouTube channel called *The Root*. When the subject of slavery and colonialism was touched upon, Professor Cooper made the following statement:

> That's what white human beings do. Prior to them, black and brown people have sailed across oceans, interacting with each other for centuries without total subjugation, domination and colonialism (Cooper, 2021).

We see here a presumably unwitting illustration of the myth of the 'noble savage'. Black and brown people never engaged in slavery or colonialism; these being sins of which white people alone can have been guilty. The irony of a woman who is evidently of Bantu heritage saying this will become apparent later in this book, when we examine the history of the Bantu conquest of sub-Saharan Africa.

This slight detour has been necessary to explain why very few people seem to realize that the slave trade in Africa was started by black people and that even when the white colonial authorities tried to suppress it from the early nineteenth century onwards, they found fierce resistance to such a move from the Africans themselves, who regarded this as an unwarranted interference in their time-honoured and traditional way of life. So determined were many Africans to maintain slavery in their countries that even by the time that Britain began to withdraw from the continent and grant independence to former colonies in the 1960s, the trade in slaves was still going strong, as indeed it is to this very day.

Not a single African country is now ruled by European colonists and yet slavery still exists. For all that American and British people are ringing their hands over the slave trade of the eighteenth and nineteenth centuries, the melancholy truth is that there are more slaves in the world today than at any time in history. In Africa, slavery is flourishing. With the removal of British prohibitions on the practice of slavery, it has enjoyed a boom since the 1960s.

In this book, we shall be looking at the history of slavery and the slave trade in Africa, which was, with few exceptions, carried out by black Africans. It was this indigenous tradition of slavery which allowed the transatlantic slave trade to flourish. Without African slavery and African slave traders, there would have been no people for the white sailors and merchants to transport across the ocean to the Americas. In short, the millions of black slaves who ended up in North and South America and the islands of the Caribbean were taken forcibly from their homes and sold into slavery not by white Europeans but rather by their fellow Africans.

Before examining the history of slavery in Africa, it might be helpful to look at the early origins of slavery in the rest of the world, which is so widespread across time and geographical space as to indicate that slavery is the closest thing we can find to a universal custom, at least until a few centuries ago.

Chapter 1

A Brief History of Slavery

Before we look at actual instances of slavery, it might be helpful to think a little about the nature of the thing. Many of us draw upon our ideas of slavery from a stock of images acquired from films such as *12 Years a Slave*. Sometimes, our vision of slavery is influenced by fictional works such as either the film or book of *Gone With the Wind* or perhaps older works such as *Uncle Tom's Cabin*. This is unfortunate, because it gives us a very distorted and unrealistic idea of the institution. All three of these accounts are of course fictional. Although *12 Years a Slave* was heavily promoted as being based upon a true account of slavery in the southern states of America before the American Civil War, the book upon which it was based was actually written by a white man called David Wilson (Northup, 1853). It is no more an authentic vision of slavery than *Gone With the Wind* or *Uncle Tom's Cabin*, both of which were written by white women.

Of course, it is quite true that some slaves in the Caribbean or the southern states of America were kept in dreadful conditions, whipped and mistreated while labouring as field hands on cotton plantations for instance, but that is not the full story by any means. For others, life was little different from what it would have been if those concerned had been ordinary citizens.

In the Introduction, mention was made of Olaudah Equiano. He was originally taken prisoner as a child by African slavers, who sold him to a black family. Eventually, he was traded on to white slave traders and taken across the Atlantic. Equiano ended up being bought by a wealthy Quaker merchant in the West Indies called Robert King, and by Equiano's own account his working life with King was almost indistinguishable from how it would have been had he been a free employee, rather than a slave.

> I had the good fortune to please my master in every department in which he employed me; and there was scarcely any part of his business, or household affairs, in which I was not occasionally engaged. I often supplied the place of a clerk, in receiving and delivering cargoes to the ships, in tending stores, and delivering goods (Equiano, 1789).

Robert King even trusted his slave to take voyages overseas on business to other parts of the Caribbean. If this strikes us today as an odd way to treat somebody who was technically a slave, this only goes to show how little we know about the way that slavery has operated over the centuries. A contemporary portrait of Olaudah Equiano is shown in Illustration 3.

Other slaves in the past have risen to be the right-hand men of kings and to wield the most extraordinary power. The Biblical story of Joseph, who became virtually the ruler of Egypt, may be apocryphal but accurately depicts the heights to which some slaves might aspire. In Greece and Rome, as well as the Muslim world, slaves were sometimes more important than free men and often treated as being members of the families which owned them. In the Ottoman Empire, slaves became Grand Viziers of the Sultan, roughly equivalent to the post of Prime Minister in the modern world. Some slaves in the classical world were granted, or managed to purchase, their freedom and there is no suggestion that their former condition was ever held against them in their subsequent lives as free men. A recently-discovered instance of this in the Roman world illustrates the point perfectly.

In August 2021 the tomb of an adult man was uncovered at Pompei, the Roman town buried when the volcano Vesuvius erupted in 79 AD. There were two noteworthy and remarkable things about the tomb. The first was that it contained the partially mummified body of an adult. Most adults at that time were cremated and it was, in general, only the bodies of children which were buried intact in this way. This suggests that the person in the tomb was very important and probably exceedingly wealthy too, judging by the decoration of his final resting-place (*Guardian*, 2021). There was something even more extraordinary about the burial though, because the name of the man interred was already familiar from some ancient archives. His name was Marcus Venerius Secundio and he had at one time been a slave.

The name of Marcus Venerius Secundio is listed on a wax tablet in the records of Caecilius Iucundus, a banker in Pompei. He is identified as a slave. Yet at some point he acquired his freedom and became so successful in Roman society that his family were able to provide him with the grandest tomb which has yet been unearthed in Pompei. There is no reason to suppose that in his later life, the fact that he had once been a slave counted against him either in his career or social life. This easy transition from being a slave to becoming a free citizen was by no means uncommon in the classical world.

It is important to bear in mind that the status of slaves could vary enormously, from place to place and time to time. This is especially the case when considering slavery in Africa. It is often suggested that slavery in Africa should not be thought of as being in the same category as that which was practised in the Western World and we shall have more to say of this later. For now, it is enough to observe that the condition of slavery, that is to say the compulsory and uncompensated servitude of one person towards another, is not one single type of existence, but consists rather of a spectrum ranging from hideous cruelty at one end to almost limitless power and the highest honour at the other.

Some human activities have, from the beginning of recorded history, been regarded as undesirable and best avoided by respectable people. Theft is one example of this and so is having sexual relations with somebody else's husband or wife. Giving false testimony in support of legal proceedings is another of those things which have been frowned upon in all civilizations from the earliest times. What has become known as the Code of Hammurabi, a table of laws promulgated in Babylon around 1750 BC, sets out the penalties for such offences as perjury, theft and arson, all three of which are of course still regarded in the modern world as being reprehensible (Davison, 1992). The Bible contains much the same system of laws relating to civil matters, which may be found in the books of Deuteronomy and Leviticus. One practice which most people in the modern world view with detestation and horror though is not condemned either in the Bible nor in the Code of Hammurabi. Slavery is mentioned in both legal systems and various regulations about it are set out, but the idea itself of buying and selling human beings as though they were cattle is accepted as being unremarkable. The Code of Hammurabi, for instance, mandates the death penalty for those who harbour or aid a runaway slave, making it plain that this offence is seen as being on a level with receiving stolen property (Epstein, 1959).

That slavery was taken for granted in the ancient Middle East, including Babylon and Israel, probably had something to do with the antiquity of the practice. We know that slavery had already been a normal part of everyday life in southern Mesopotamia, where the Babylonian Empire arose, for centuries before Hammurabi devised his table of laws. The earliest recorded mention of the trade in slaves is to be found in a small sun-baked clay tablet excavated a century ago at Nippur, in what is now Iraq. The inscription listed laws drawn up by the Sumerian king Ur-Nammu, who ruled from 2112 to 2095 BC. There are several references to slaves and it is clear by the context that these were treated as chattels, like sheep or cattle (Cotterell, 1980). These laws antedate those of Hammurabi by 300 years or so.

One common feature which may be seen in slavery in ancient times, and then as a continuing thread through to the present, is that there has from the earliest times been a preference for slaves to be drawn from nations or ethnicities other than that of the society which makes use of them. Whether they were seized during bouts of warfare or captured during raids on territory belonging to somebody else, the outsider always made a more desirable and acceptable slave than somebody who shared a common language, religion and culture with the owner. Even when members of the majority society *were* made slaves, through debt bondage for instance, different rules almost invariably applied to them.

This concept of the slave being ideally an outsider was explicitly stated in the Middle East almost 4,000 years ago and was considered so important that it was codified into both civil and religious law. The laws of Hammurabi, for instance, of which mention was made above, required that after three years of servitude a slave who was a fellow countryman should be freed. This freeing of slaves who belong to the same nation as the owner, a process known as manumission, was also commanded in the Jewish scriptures. In Exodus, the second book of the Torah and also of course part of the Old Testament, Hebrew slaves owned by another Hebrew must be freed after six years.

It is this general feeling, that people are more comfortable if their slaves are in some sense 'others', which may be seen time and again in the history of slavery and the slave trade. Sometimes, it is explicitly stated and set down as a dictate of religion, but more generally it has simply been an unremarked fact. We feel less uneasy about enslaving or mistreating foreigners or people who belong to a different religion from us than we do about keeping slaves with whom we share a common culture.

It was not only in the Middle East that slavery was a common and unremarkable feature of life thousands of years ago. In India, slavery was certainly widespread at the beginning of the Common Era and was probably around at least as early as the time of the Buddha, in the seventh century BC (Singh, 2009). Slavery in China is thought to have existed from the time of the earliest culture, the Shang dynasty, which began around 1700 BC and lasted for 700 years (Cotterell, 1980). It is a little more difficult to say anything definite about the situation in North and South America, because of the paucity of written history from that part of the world before the coming of Europeans. We know that the Maya enslaved captured enemies (Coe and Houston, 2015) and so did the Aztecs. The suggestion is sometimes made that it was white European settlers who introduced slavery to the North American continent, but this is quite untrue. Just as in the rest of the world, the capture in battle or kidnapping of members of other tribes or ethnic groups resulted in slavery. Two especially enterprising tribes from the modern territory of Alaska provide an example of how this system operated. The Haida and Tlingit raided for slaves all the way along the Pacific coast of what is now the United States, to such effect that it has been estimated that in some parts of the north-west Pacific coast, as much a quarter of the population were slaves (MacDonald, 1996).

It is in Europe where we have the most information about slavery as it was operating thousands of years ago. This is for the obvious reason that the Greek and Roman civilizations were literate and left extensive records of the minute details of slavery, including descriptions of the acquisition and trade in slaves. Combining such writings with archaeological investigation allows us to build up an accurate picture of slavery in Europe in the centuries preceding and following the birth of Christ.

The earliest attestation to the existence of slavery in Europe is almost as old as that which saw earlier from Sumer. In the 1950s an archaic form of written Greek known as Linear B was first deciphered and it was found that on clay tablets recording commercial transactions of the sale of grain, wine and other commodities, slaves were also mentioned as being bought and sold (Rodriguez, 1997). These tablets date back to 1450 BC (Robinson, 2002). Other than the simple fact that there were slaves in that part of the Eastern Mediterranean at that time, these translated lists tell us little more. Reading Greek literature from 1,000 years or so later fleshes out the picture. Homer's *Odyssey*, although fiction, portrays a world where slaves are treated, and behave, as part of the family (Homer, 1987).

It is impossible to say just how many slaves there were in the Greek city-states 2,500 years ago at the time that Socrates and Plato were teaching and writing. One estimate is that there might have been 100,000 slaves altogether in the peninsula of Attica, the area which included Athens. This would mean that perhaps a quarter of the people living in that part of the Mediterranean were slaves (Andrewes, 1971). In some of the Greek city-states the proportion was much higher than in others. In Sparta, the free men were, according to the historian Herodotus, outnumbered seven to one by the slaves known as Helots. These were the descendants of those who had once lived in the vicinity of Sparta in the territories of Laconia and Messenia. It is significant that when Plato set out to imagine an idealized society in *The Republic*, he could only come up with a nation in which slaves were an integral part of the social order (Plato, 2007). It was unthinkable for an educated Athenian of the fifth century BC that menial tasks should have been undertaken by free citizens.

It was in the Roman Empire that slavery reached its greatest extent in Europe and the surrounding territories. In its early years, it is thought that there might have been as many as 10,000,000 slaves, making up between a fifth and a sixth of the population (D'Arms and Kopf, 1980). The scale of the slave trade in Europe at that time is quite staggering. It has been calculated that in the city of Rome alone, there were something like 400,000 slaves, who made up a third of the population (Davison, 1992). Because the life expectancy of these slaves was very low – males might, on average expect to live to the age of 17.2 years and females 17.9 (Harper, 1972) – the turnover was very high and new slaves had constantly to be acquired. To maintain the same number of slaves, upon whose labour the empire was so dependent, required the capture of many thousands of new slaves each year (D'Arms and Kopf, 1980).

The custom of slavery was not confined to those areas under Roman control. Before the conquest of Britain, the island was known to be a centre for the slave trade. Writing in about 10 AD, the Greek geographer Strabo had this to say of the economy of Britain at that time.

> It bears grain, cattle, gold, silver, and iron. These things, accordingly, are exported from the island, as also hides, and slaves, and dogs that are by nature suited to the purposes of the chase (Strabo, 1923).

Not that we need just take the word of a writer from a couple of thousand years ago for this; we have archaeological evidence to show that slavery was operating in Britain before the Roman occupation. Iron 'gang chains' have been found in Britain which were in use centuries before the arrival of the Romans. When the RAF were constructing a runway on the Welsh island of Anglesey during the Second World War, they dredged a small lake called Llyn Cerrig and among other bits and pieces came upon a long chain (Williams, 2006). It was in such good condition that it was put to use by the airmen. Some cars had become stuck in the mud which surrounded the lake and the newly-discovered iron chain was hooked behind a tractor and used to haul them back onto dry land.

The chain pulled out of Llyn Cerrig was later dated to some 300 years before the Roman invasion of Britain and had been designed to link five people together by metal collars which would have been fastened around their necks. It is the kind of thing which was used in other parts of the world to ensure that slaves were not in a position to slip away when they were not being watched. It would have been possible to secure one end of the chain to an immovable object like a tree. A similar set of chains from the same period were unearthed at Bigbury Camp near Canterbury. These had leg shackles which were long enough to allow a slave to shuffle along, but would prevent him or her from running or even walking briskly.

Slavery became even more widespread in Britain during the Roman occupation, which lasted for 400 years or so. Iron shackles have been found from this time, as well as little statuettes depicting bound slaves. In 2021, news emerged of the starkest evidence yet of the existence of slavery in England during the period when that part of Europe was under Roman rule. During the construction of a conservatory at a house in the Midlands village of Great Casterton, a skeleton was found. The police were notified, but it soon became apparent that this was no recent murder victim. The ankles of the skeleton, which was later carbon-dated to between AD 226 to AD 427 (*Guardian*, 2021), were linked by rusty iron shackles. Examination showed that this had been a man aged between 25 and 35 and that he had led an arduous and physically demanding life. After his death, the corpse had simply been tossed into a ditch as though it were a thing of little worth.

After the Romans left, the Celts continued to keep slaves and the Angles, Saxons, Jutes and Vikings who came to live in the country were also keen on the institution of slavery. When the Domesday Book was compiled from information gathered in 1086, it was found that about a tenth of the English population were slaves (Trevelyan, 1942).

It is interesting to note that slavery in Africa was to be the lot of many people in England between the end of the Roman occupation and the Norman Conquest in 1066. The Vikings raided England more or less with impunity for many years, carrying off anything of value which took their fancy. This ranged from silver and gold ornaments from monasteries to young people who could be sold as slaves. In Ireland the Vikings set up special camps devoted to slave trading, rather like the forts which Europeans later set up for the same purpose in West Africa. Over the course of time, these grew to be towns and then cities. Dublin was founded in this way as a slave-trading centre in 841 AD (Haywood, 2008). In time it became a major city; its prosperity and growth though were inextricably bound up with the trade in slaves (Cunliffe *et al*, 2001). The Irish cities of Limerick and Waterford had similar origins. Slaves were collected from various parts of Europe and brought to these centres, where they were sold to slave dealers who would export them to different parts of the world, including

Scandinavia and North Africa. It will perhaps come as a surprise to modern readers to learn that English slaves sold in Dublin at this time, the centuries leading up to the Norman Conquest, were being bought by dealers who took them to Africa. Even more surprising will perhaps be the route by which they reached Dublin.

In the summer of 2020 the English city of Bristol was one focus for protests intended to support the Black Lives Matter movement. These took place in the aftermath of the death of a black man in America following his arrest. Bristol seemed a logical place for feelings to run high about the treatment of black people, because of course the city had been, centuries earlier, a centre for the transatlantic slave trade. The well-known historian Asa Briggs stated bluntly that Bristol 'was the main English port involved in Triangular Trade' (Briggs, 1983). It was perhaps inevitable that it was here that the demonstrations against the past history of slavery reached a crescendo, leading to the toppling of the statue of a man who had once been involved in the slave trade. What was odd though was that it was only one particular type of slave trade which exercised the minds of the protestors and that was of course *the* slave trade; which is to say the transatlantic slave trade. Bristol's connection with the slave trade and Africa though had been thriving hundreds of years before the birth of the man whose statue was so unceremoniously dumped in Bristol's harbour in 2020.

When the Vikings and other slavers were at work in England, buying or seizing people who could be exported and sold for a profit, they needed a handy port from which they could be taken to the major slave-trading centre of Dublin. Bristol fitted the bill perfectly and it was to this city that many of the slave caravans made their way across England (Rodgers, 2007). The scene in Bristol is described by a contemporary writer in the early eleventh century.

> You could see and sigh over rows of wretches bound together with ropes, young people of both sexes whose beautiful

appearance and youthful innocence might move barbarians to pity, daily exposed to prostitution, daily offered for sale (Pelteret, 2001).

This account was set down over 600 years before the birth of Edward Colston, the man whose statue was toppled in 2020. It shows that long before it became a centre concerned with the exporting of slaves *from* Africa, Bristol played a role in seeing slaves exported from England, first to Ireland and then *to* Africa. One cannot help but wonder how many of those people taking part in the disorders associated with the Black Lives Matter movement were aware of this.

The aim of this brief chapter has been to give an overview of slavery from the earliest times in order to show that it has been a feature of most civilizations and found on every continent. Africa was no exception to this general rule. The present focus in Britain and the United States upon the transatlantic slave trade, and attempts to portray it as *the* slave trade, has led to a distorted view of history. This trend has probably been driven in part by a very right and proper desire not to upset or offend those of African origin and to show that the countries which benefitted economically from the transatlantic slave trade, primarily Britain and America of course, regret their participation in such an awful business. This does not mean though that white people, as a whole, should feel obliged to ignore history and shoulder the entirety of the blame for what happened; merely that it is acknowledged that a number of their ancestors, like those of many black people, played a role in what happened.

Chapter 2

Slavery in North Africa in Ancient Times

Before looking at slavery in the northern part of the African continent, it might be worth making a slight etymological detour and reflecting upon the current meaning attributed to the word 'African'. We should also consider the anthropology and geography of Africa and realize that this is essentially a continent of two separate and distinct parts.

For many people, hearing the word 'African' conjures up immediately the image of a black person. 'African immigrants' are black people and an 'African' country means somewhere south of the Sahara Desert; perhaps Kenya, Uganda or Nigeria. Those from parts of Africa north of the Sahara are never referred to as Africans. Instead, they are described in terms of nationality, as Libyans, Egyptians, Moroccans and so on, or sometimes by ethnicity; Arabs or Berbers. When such people *are* referred to as Africans, it is usually to make a political statement. To make this clear, we need only think about a perennial feature of Black History Month, which takes place in Britain during October.

One of the little-known 'facts' which is routinely trotted out during Black History Month is that one Roman emperor was African. This man died in England and it is also said that African troops were garrisoned at Hadrian's Wall. Those hearing these statements assume, as a matter of course, that both the emperor and the soldiers were black. After all, why else would these 'Africans' be mentioned at all during Black History Month? In reality, of course, the emperor was from a colonial family and he was part Roman and part Phoenician. He certainly had no sub-Saharan ancestry that anybody knows of.

In the same way, the Roman soldiers guarding Hadrian's Wall were technically African and it is sometimes mentioned that they were from Mauretania. Since the modern country of Mauretania lies south of the Sahara Desert, it is naturally assumed that these African troops were black. The Roman province of Mauretania though occupied that part of North Africa which is today Morocco. The soldiers were Berber, rather than black African. It is for this reason that readers of this book, when first they picked it up, will most likely have assumed that it treated of slavery among, and involving, black people. Very possibly, they did not even consider the possibility that it covered countries which are on the fringe of the Mediterranean. Still less are they likely to have considered the possibility that some of the slaves in Africa of whom they would be reading were white English people and Americans, as well as many from Europe and even as far afield as Iceland. This is all rather curious, because the earliest records of slavery and slave-trading in Africa that we have relate to those North African countries with a Mediterranean coastline rather than that part of the continent which lies below the Sahara Desert.

North and sub-Saharan Africa should be treated as separate geographical entities because although below the Sahara has always been the homeland of nations and tribes of varying degrees of blackness, this is not at all the case for the coastal region stretching from the Atlantic Ocean in the west to Egypt in the east. From Morocco and Algeria, through Tunisia and Libya, and on to Egypt, the coast of north Africa has never been inhabited by black people. The earliest group of which we know are the light-skinned Berbers, whose descendants linger on to this day, although they have interbred with Arabs and others. As far as is known, the Berbers are the original inhabitants of North Africa (Desanges, 1990). The Berber language is associated with the Semitic languages of Hebrew and Arabic and there is no evidence to suggest that the Berbers ever displaced an indigenous population. Although the Berber language is written in an ancient script, sometimes known as 'Old Libyan' (Dalby, 1998), the only inscriptions found are short. Most of the inscriptions in Old Libyan consist of nothing more than names and there is nothing to give any information about the people who used this script.

Because there was no written history in most of sub-Saharan Africa until the arrival of Islam, the earliest records of slavery in the continent come from civilizations such as dynastic Egypt, Carthage and the Roman Republic. The mysterious Garamantes civilization of the Sahara was also heavily involved in the slave trade, according to several contemporary sources. It is generally supposed that the Garamantes were Berbers (Keys, 2004). It is Egypt though which was, until fairly recently, connected in the minds of most people in the West with slavery, for it was there that the first slavery in Africa for which we have any records is found. The reason that it was at one time the first place to spring to mind for those in Europe and the United States when mention was made of slavery is of course because until a generation or two ago, most people living in the West had at least a passing familiarity with Bible stories such as Joseph being sold into slavery by his brothers and also the way that the Hebrews laboured as slaves in Egypt before the Exodus. Illustration 4 is of the old, and fanciful, view of these events, with Hebrews building the Pyramids.

There is some dispute about the ethnic origins of the ancient Egyptians, a puzzle which modern DNA tests are beginning to unravel. For many years, it was uncertain whether the ancient Egyptians were an African people, perhaps akin to the Berbers, or had their origins outside that continent. Since the 1980s, an alternative theory has become increasingly popular, that this civilization was made up of sub-Saharan, black Africans and that their culture spread out and from Africa into Asia and Europe (Bernal, 1987). By this reading of the situation, the philosophers and mathematicians of Greece, people like Euclid and Plato, owed their intellectual achievements to black Africans. Although few serious archaeologists adhere to this theory, it is undeniably true that many Egyptians today look as though they have at least some black ancestry. In the former president of the country,

Anwar Sadat, who was assassinated in 1981, this heritage was so marked that it was the object of contemptuous remark by his political opponents. He was sometimes referred to by a slang expression which amounted to a racial slur associated with black people.

It was only with the advent of accurate DNA testing that it became possible to solve the conundrum of Egyptian origins. Samples were taken from a number of mummies covering a period of some 1,300 years, roughly from 1000 BC up to the third century AD (Schuenemann *et al*, 2017). The results were conclusive. The ancestry of those tested lay not in sub-Saharan Africa but rather in the Middle East. Specifically, the families of these individuals had their origins in Turkey and the Eastern Mediterranean. They were of Semitic stock. This ties in neatly with what we know of the language spoken in ancient Egypt, which belongs to a group known as Afro-Asiatic. This group of languages includes Hebrew, Arabic, Old Egyptian and also Berber (Dalby, 1998). It can be said with assurance that the rulers of the earliest kingdom in dynastic Egypt were more closely connected with the Semites of what is sometimes known as the Fertile Crescent than they were with the black Africans who lived south of the Sahara Desert.

As was remarked above, when churchgoing was more regular and widespread than is now the case in Britain and the United States, most people knew about the Hebrew bondage in Egypt and how Moses led his people to freedom. This became muddled up in people's minds with monumental architecture such as the Pyramids and the idea arose that many of the splendid temples and tombs of ancient Egypt had been constructed by slave labour. Illustration 4 neatly sums up this misconception. Modern scholars now regard this as improbable. This is because careful examination of the towns where those who built the Pyramids lived reveals that they were not held in captivity at all. In fact, when such workers died, they were accorded the honour of a burial alongside the royal tomb. This would have been an unheard-of honour for slaves. The evidence for this new reading of the past began to emerge in the early years of the twenty-first century (Reuters, 2010) and has since been confirmed by archaeological excavations (Sowada, 2018).

The Great Pyramid, the epitome of monumental architecture in ancient Egypt, was constructed around 2500 BC. It was another thousand years before slavery became a feature of Egyptian civilization. This was during the time of the so-called New Kingdom, which lasted from 1500 to 1175 BC, give or take a few centuries (Hawkes, 1973). The reason that slavery did not feature to any great extent before this time was simple. The structure of society in Egypt was similar in some ways to that of the feudal system in medieval Europe. Peasants could be drafted to undertake work when required by the aristocracy and sometimes this forced labour was very similar to slavery. For this reason, ancient Egyptian civilization had no real need for slaves. It could 'have been created and maintained without them' (Hawkes, 1973).

Slaves were not needed for heavy work such as building pyramids or temples since the peasantry could easily be impressed into service for such projects. However, slaves were acquired for special tasks as artisans: weavers, tailors, cooks and so on. Just as in most other cultures, the preferred means of procuring slaves was to seize foreigners, either in war or during raids with the specific aim of taking captives. Because the River Nile, with its fertile banks, stretched down into Africa, the most convenient source of slaves consisted of black people from Nubia, the area south of Egypt which is today known as Sudan. There are a number of paintings and sculptures which show black slaves in Egypt. One such may be seen in Illustration 5. The acquisition of black slaves from Africa who were imported into Egypt increased as the Ptolemies, Greek rulers, came to power in the country (Bradley and Cartledge, 2011). It is from these slaves that the black ancestry of modern Egyptians comes, along with the other slaves brought to Egypt later, after the Arab conquest of North Africa.

Another civilization in North Africa which made use of black slaves was Carthage. Some time after 1000 BC a Phoenician colony was established on the coast of what is now Tunisia. The Phoenicians came from the Middle East: their homeland was north of Israel, where the country of Lebanon now is. The Phoenicians were great sailors and explorers, and it has been suggested that they were the first to circumnavigate Africa. They settled various territories in the Mediterranean, including Sicily and Spain (Cotterell, 1980). These colonies were part of the Phoenician empire, although in the course of time the colony of Carthage grew in importance until it eclipsed Phoenicia itself, becoming a separate power entirely. From this city, the Carthaginians began to build an empire of their own which stretched across much of North Africa and also extended to Spain, Sicily, Corsica and Sardinia, absorbing these former Phoenician colonies as their own (Cotterell, 1980).

Like almost every other nation of the time, Carthage was a slave-owning society. Perhaps because the Phoenicians who had originally founded Carthage were such great international traders, the Carthaginians tended to acquire their slaves by buying them, rather than going to the trouble of hunting for them and taking them prisoner themselves. The people from whom Carthage purchased slaves were almost certainly a little-known nation called the Garamantes.

Before looking at the Garamantes and their origins, a word or two might not come amiss about the barrier which was mentioned above as dividing Africa into two distinct geographical and ethnic areas. This is the Sahara Desert, which even today serves as a barrier to the free movement of populations. It was not of course always so. Scattered across the world's largest desert are mute witnesses to the fact that this was not always the harsh, arid and inhospitable place that we know today. In some places are hollowed-out stones and boulders, usually with smooth and rounded cobblestones laying nearby. These are quern stones that were used over 5,000 years ago to grind the seeds of wild grasses into a primitive kind of flour, presumably to bake into bread. Needless to say, there is little today in the way of wild grasses growing in that part of the world.

The quern stones found in the Sahara were being used at roughly the same time as various rock paintings and engravings were being made, which showed giraffes, lions and domesticated cattle. It seems that at one time the Sahara Desert was more like the savannah to the south. We can say little about the people who lived here at that time, but by about 1000 BC they had vanished, giving way to another ethnic group whose origins were to the north and east.

As the savannah dried up and slowly turned to the desert which we know today, the nomadic pastoralists whose herds of cattle once lived there moved south into central Africa. As they did so, a new ethnic group living on the coast of the Mediterranean began to move south. These people are the ancestors of the present-day Berbers and in the last few years study of the genome of modern populations in North Africa has revealed some surprising facts. Although there is little or no trace of black ancestry before the Arab invasion of the seventh and eighth centuries, there is certainly reason to suppose that outsiders influenced events in that part of Africa thousands of years ago. There is what one study calls 'long-term genetic continuity in the region' (Fregel et al, 2018), especially in what is now Morocco, and there is also reason to suppose that there was a wave of invasion from an unexpected direction in about 1000 BC. Writing 45 years ago, one researcher had already concluded that this was likely to be the case: 'By 1000 BC, these racial migrations had led to the establishment of the Hamitic and Semitic-speaking Eurasian tribes' (Lhote, 1977).

The testing of the genomes of modern Berbers shows precisely this, that Europeans and people from the Middle East migrated to North Africa, bringing with them not only their genetic inheritance but also their languages. Berber has little connection with languages south of the Sahara, but is associated more with Hebrew and Arabic. The most surprising discovery when examining the Berber DNA was that there seems to be some affinity with the Sami tribes of Lapland.

These discoveries also go some way towards explaining how it was that horses entered the equation at some point. We remember that

Herodotus talked of horse-drawn chariots and we know that horses are not native to Africa. The only possibility is that they were introduced from Europe, via the Middle East. It is time to make the acquaintance of these horse soldiers, who are known as the Garamantes.

Few people, other than historians and archaeologists, are likely to have heard of the Garamantes. The members of this culture belonged to the indigenous inhabitants of North Africa, those who were living there before the Phoenicians, Romans and Arabs variously colonized that part of the African continent over a period of some 1,700 years. Their descendants today are thought to be the Berbers and Tuareg.

The Garamantes thrived in parts of what is now Libya and also other areas of North Africa. The first written mention of them is found in the work of Herodotus, the Greek historian. Writing in the fifth century BC, Herodotus described the Garamantes as a great nation who kept cattle and farmed dates (Herodotus, 2003). He also said that they hunted Ethiopians by means of horse-drawn chariots. This is interesting, because there are indeed rock paintings from the Sahara made long ago which show cattle herding, the collection of dates and also men riding in chariots. We see a chariot shown from a rock painting in the Sahara made at that time in Illustration 6. As for hunting Ethiopians, a term often used in antiquity as a general term for black people from sub-Saharan African, there are good grounds for supposing this to be true. It is strongly suspected that the Garamantes made raids across the Sahara in search of slaves to sell to Carthaginian settlements (Law, 1967) and certain that they did so to enslave Africans of their own to undertake heavy manual work. Once the Romans had dislodged the Carthaginians and colonized the Mediterranean coast of Africa for themselves, the Garamantes sold slaves to them as well.

The Romans had a fractious relationship with the Garamantes, fighting with them at one point and later buying slaves from them. These slaves were black Africans whom the Garamantes had crossed the Sahara to take prisoner. The use of the wheel was unknown in sub-

Saharan Africa at that time, perhaps 50 or 100 AD, and the sight of the Garamantes bearing down on them in their chariots must have been a terrifying one to the inhabitants of Mali, one part of Africa from which slaves were taken. There is mention in Roman writings of the Imperial Era of the black slaves bought from the Garamantes (Law, 1967).

The Romans may have been eager to buy slaves in North Africa, but there is no evidence that they took them to Europe. It is possible to gauge roughly the ethnic origin of human skeletons by measuring the proportions of the skull. By analysing the enamel of the teeth and measuring the presence or absence of various isotopes, it can also be discovered where an individual was born and spent his or her childhood. It has been estimated that between a third and four-tenths of the population of Rome 2,000 years ago consisted of slaves (Davison, 1992). These men, women and children tended to be buried in unremarkable graves, very different from the elaborate tombs of the wealthy and important. One cemetery for such lower-status people was excavated and the teeth studied. This was the necropolis of Isola Sacra, near Rome. It was discovered that many of those buried there had been born and spent their childhoods in other parts of Europe, which suggested that they may well have been slaves who had been captured and brought to Rome. Of the sixty-one bodies examined, only one had elements in its teeth consistent with having grown up outside Europe; namely in north Africa (Prowse *et al*, 2007). Whatever slaves the Garamantes acquired in sub-Saharan African and then sold to the Romans seemingly remained in Africa.

In addition to trading in black slaves and selling them to successive colonial powers on the Mediterranean coast of Africa, the Garamantes also made extensive use of slave labour themselves for their quarrying projects. Water on the fringes of the Sahara Desert is a rare and precious commodity and there is scarcely enough rainfall to maintain a great nation in the southern parts of Libya, where the Garamantes were chiefly based. They struck though upon an inexhaustible source of fresh water in this arid zone, albeit one which was very heavily labour-intensive to exploit.

The Sahara Desert and the countries surrounding it were not always parched and desperately short of water. Thousands of years ago, the area was lush and green, as attested to by the archaeological remains found, together with the rock paintings showing pastoral scenes. At that time, rain was plentiful and there was abundant water for agriculture. When the region became desert, much of the water which had fallen stayed where it was, locked up in underground caverns and tunnels in the sandstone which stretched across Egypt, Libya and Sudan. What is now known as the Nubian Sandstone Aquifer System covers over two million square kilometres. The water trapped in the rocks is sometimes called fossil water, having fallen as rain between 4,000 and 20,000 years ago (*National Geographic*, 2010).

Starting in perhaps 600 BC, the Garamantes began to extract fossil water from the sandstones which surrounded them, by digging tunnels and shafts to tap the many aquifers which lay beneath the surface (Mattingly, 2003). Perhaps it is not strictly speaking accurate to say that the Garamantes dug the shafts. They rather used gangs of black African slaves to carry out these excavations; the remains of both tunnels and slaves may still be seen to this day. Although it seems from rock paintings and other evidence that the Garamantes once inhabited a large part of the Sahara Desert in the days before it was actually a desert, once it began to dry up they moved north and established a homeland in the south of Libya. They soon found that there was limitless water, if only enough mining could be undertaken.

The fossil water in Fezzan, which is what this part of Africa is now called, lies about 120ft beneath the ground, so a great deal of work was needed before it could be reached and extracted in sufficient quantities to support an entire nation (Gearon, 2011). Fortunately for the Garamantes though, they had long-established routes across the desert to central and west Africa. They obtained gold and slaves from these parts and it was upon such expeditions that the prosperity of the Garamantes was founded.

When the former capital of the Garamantes was the subject of archaeological examination, a good deal of light was shed on those who had lived there and their origins. Excavations in Garama, which is today called Germa, have uncovered an astonishing 120,000 graves. It has from this been deduced that the city and surrounding towns supported a population of perhaps 10,000 people at its height (Gearon, 2011). An interesting point was that many graves contained Nubian artefacts, confirming the extensive contact which the Garamantes had with black African tribes. As has already been said, the Garamantes themselves were almost certainly Berbers, the light-skinned peoples who lived in North Africa before the Carthaginians, Romans and Arabs. Measurement of the skulls found suggested that a lot of those buried in Garama had been black. Since the whole of the Garamantes' civilization and culture depended ultimately, as is still the case with all modern cultures, on the provision of fresh water, we can perhaps say that the Garamantes of Fezzan were an African people wholly reliant upon slave labour for their very existence. Illustration 8 shows an Egyptian depiction of Nubian slaves of the kind which the Garamantes both made use of themselves and also sold to their neighbours.

The picture of at least part of Africa which we have outlined in this chapter is perhaps a little surprising to the modern reader. Those who have been gulled into the belief that slavery is in some way an invention of Europe will have been surprised to find that the practice was indigenous to North Africa from the earliest times of which we have any record. Slavery existed there before any contact with Europe and was later maintained by various colonial occupiers, only one of whom, the Romans, was European. What of sub-Saharan Africa though? Was slavery something which was inflicted upon them only by outsiders, whether from Egypt, Rome, Carthage or the Arab world? In the next chapter we turn our attention to black Africa and the evidence for indigenous slavery there. Before doing so, however, it is necessary to touch upon part of the Roman slave trade which took place far from North Africa, in what are now the countries of Tanzania and Kenya.

The Romans may have bought slaves from the Garamantes, but that would inevitably inflate the price, to include a profit for the middlemen in the enterprise. In Europe and Asia though, the Romans cheerfully captured their own slaves in vast numbers. It has been suggested that at its height, the Roman Empire required half a million new slaves each year (D'Arms and Kopf, 1980). These came from Northern Europe and the fringes of other parts of the empire. In North Africa the Romans felt no need in general to wage war or make raids to acquire slaves. The easiest way of getting hold of them was simply to buy them. Mounting raids across the Sahara Desert and into Central Africa would have required serious planning and large amounts of manpower. Far simpler just to trade with the Garamantes, the people who undertook the raids. There was one part of sub-Saharan Africa though where the Romans seemed to have maintained a presence of some kind, although it was never part of the empire. This was the area known later as the Swahili Coast.

In a later chapter, we shall be examining in detail the slave trade which took place from East Africa to other parts of the world; a trade not nearly as widely known of as that from West Africa. This was focussed around the coast near the island of Zanzibar and was conducted by both Arabs and Portuguese colonists, together with African slavers. There was an earlier episode of slave trading from this part of Africa, however, and it involved some very adventurous Roman merchants who were prepared to travel many hundreds of miles from the borders of their empire in order to take part in a very profitable business. There are two strands of evidence for this activity, by far the southernmost influence of Rome of which we know.

The *Periplus of the Erythraean Sea* is a document composed by an unknown author, which was written in Greek and probably dates from the middle of the first century AD. It details trading centres and navigational routes along the Red Sea, the Horn of Africa and as far south as what are now Kenya, Tanzania and the island of Zanzibar. The descriptions given are very precise and the goods mentioned, notably ivory and slaves, are the very ones which we know were later exported from this part of Africa (Casson, 1989). It has needed a good deal of work to be certain which ports and parts of the coast are being described in the *Periplus of the Erythraean Sea*, but historians are reasonably sure that they have been able to identify specific locations in the Horn of Africa, the east coast of Africa and even Pakistan. The most southerly of these places was Rhapta, which seems to have been a little to the south of present-day Dar es Salaam, the capital of Tanzania.

From all that can be apprehended, Romans did not make any attempt to colonize the ports on the African coast. They were, after all, traders and merchants, not soldiers. They wished only to make advantageous business deals with the local people, buying whatever they had to sell and then taking it north to dispose of at a profit. Lists of the goods which came out of East Africa are given. For instance, this passage has been identified with Ras Hafun in Somalia and reads as follows.

> And then, after sailing four hundred stadia along a promontory, toward which place the current also draws you, there is another market-town called Opone, into which the same things are imported as those already mentioned, and in it the greatest quantity of cinnamon is produced, (the arebo and moto), and slaves of the better sort, which are brought to Egypt in increasing numbers; and a great quantity of tortoiseshell, better than that found elsewhere. (Schoff, 1912)

There is archaeological evidence to support the idea that this was a place with which the Romans were familiar, because both Roman and Egyptian pottery has been unearthed here. It is known that black slaves from this part of Africa were actually being traded in Egypt at the time that this document was produced. Nor is this the only mention of the slave trade in Somalia. We also find the following:

> After Avalites there is another market-town, better than this, called Malao, distant a sail of about eight hundred stadia. The anchorage is an open roadstead, sheltered by a spit running out from the east. Here the natives are more peaceable. There are imported into this place the things already mentioned, and many tunics, cloaks from Arsinoe, dressed and dyed; drinking-cups, sheets of soft copper in small quantity, iron, and gold and silver coin, not much. There are exported from these places myrrh, a little frankincense, (that known as far-side), the harder cinnamon, duaca, Indian copal and macir, which are imported into Arabia; and slaves, but rarely. (Schoff, 1912)

Both these entries in the *Periplus of the Erythraean Sea* and others tell us unambiguously that Roman businessmen were collecting slaves from East Africa and shipping them north along the Red Sea to Egypt. By implication, it tells us too that there must have been a flourishing slave trade among the black Africans themselves. The Romans and Arabs who visited and made bases in those parts would hardly have been able to go off and capture men and women for themselves; that would have required a military expedition. Rather, they traded goods which they brought down from Egypt and North Africa; things which the Africans would desire but were unable to manufacture or obtain for themselves.

The great trick of slaving has always been to ensure that ships do not cross hundreds or thousands of miles of ocean empty. This was the essential point about what became known as the Triangular Trade in the eighteenth century, that at no stage were ships ploughing uselessly through the waves, but at all times were carrying either slaves, raw materials or manufactured goods from one place to another. This way of proceeding was, from the very earliest days of the maritime slave trade, something of a leitmotif and we see here the first iteration of that commercial method.

That the Romans carried on their trade further south than Somalia is all but certain, for Roman coins have been found on Pemba Island, which is part of the Zanzibar archipelago (Miller, 1969). Near Dar es Salaam, there have been many discoveries of Roman trade goods, which were presumably brought along the route from Egypt which passed along the Red Sea and to which the *Periplus of the Erythraean Sea* refers (Chami, 2002)

We have seen that slavery was a thriving business in North Africa 2,000 or more years ago and that most of the slaves were bought, rather than captured directly. The Garamantes actually travelled down south of the Sahara Desert and hunted black people as though they were animals, but this was very much the exception. In the main, slaves were acquired by the Egyptians, Carthaginians and Romans by the simple expedient of purchasing them. This of course leads us to ask who actually captured the slaves for whom the Roman traders exchanged the goods which they had brought south with them? The answer to this simple question is an unpalatable one in the modern era. We find that long before anybody from Europe set foot south of the Sahara, Africans, like the rest of the world, had for many years been busily engaged in enslaving one another and using men and women captured in battles or raids as chattels or belongings with which they might do as they pleased. It is time to look at slavery and the slave trade in sub-Saharan Africa.

Chapter 3

Slavery in Sub-Saharan Africa up to the Sixteenth Century

Before examining specific details relating to slavery as it operated in those parts of Africa south of the Sahara Desert, long before Europeans became involved in the continent's affairs, it might be helpful to remind readers of something which was said earlier. This is that wherever slavery has been practised, there has at all times and in all places been a preference for enslaving those who belong to a group different in language, religion, skin colour or ethnicity. Africa was, and indeed still is, no exception to this general rule. It is though sometimes a little more difficult for Europeans to understand how this principle applies in Africa, because all that the average person knows of the matter is that those living in sub-Saharan Africa are usually black. That they are divided up into many different ethnicities is not immediately apparent to the casual observer. For this reason, a slight detour into the history of anthropology as it affects sub-Saharan Africa is necessary.

Around 2500 BC, a large group of tribes from what is now Ukraine migrated west and south from their homeland, populating Europe and India (Mallory, 1989). We know these people today as the Indo-Europeans and they took with them their language, upon which all but two or three European languages, to say nothing of Indian languages like Punjabi and Hindi, are now based. After the Indo-Europeans split into groups such as the Celts, Slavs, Romans and Greeks, these various peoples began to think of themselves as being different from others whom they came across and therefore thought it acceptable to enslave them. Romans enslaved Celts, Vikings enslaved Slavs and so on. A precisely similar process took place in Africa and the after-effects of these ancient migrations last to this day.

At roughly the same time that the Indo-Europeans were moving to Europe and the Indian subcontinent, a distinct ethnic group lived in what is now Cameroon and Nigeria. These people, like the Indo-Europeans, shared a common language. Also like the Indo-Europeans, they began spreading out from their homeland and colonizing other territories, until they dominated the entire African continent. They were the Bantu-speaking tribes of West Africa, the name of whose language has become synonymous with their ethnicity (Haywood, 2008). The reason for this sudden expansion probably has something to do with the adoption by the Bantu of a settled, agricultural lifestyle. In Africa 5,000 years ago, most people were hunter-gatherers. This lifestyle, of hunting for game and collecting wild fruit, nuts and roots, requires a fairly large range, which typically means that any given area is likely to be sparsely populated. Settled and well-fed populations need less space to live, but tend to increase at a greater rate and so naturally require more land as time passes.

In appearance, the Bantu are what many people think of when they hear mention of 'black Africans'. If we imagine somebody from the modern country of Nigeria or Ghana, this tells us roughly what the Bantu looked like. The more African ancestry they have, the more that people of Caribbean heritage, African-Americans and other black people in the Western World resemble the Bantu. For most of us, this is the default setting when we think of black people. As we shall see, there is more to this than meets the eye.

The evidence suggests that between 3000 and 2500 BC the Bantu began cultivating yams, that is to say planting and harvesting them, thus establishing farming as a way of life. These people had no understanding of fertilizers or the depletion of nutrients in soil that has been cultivated for a year or two. All they knew was that fresh land grew bigger yams, which meant tilling new fields every few years. So it was that after a few centuries, the Bantu began moving south and east from their ancestral homeland, which led them in one direction into the rainforests of central Africa and in the other to the savannahs of the south. There, they came into contact with the two other major ethnic groups which inhabited sub-Saharan Africa at that time.

The greater part of Africa in 2500 BC was divided between the people we now think of as Pygmies and also the Khoi, sometimes known as 'Bushmen', although the expression is now regarded as impolite and verging on the offensive. The Pygmies, who were considerably small than the Bantu, lived in the vast forests which covered Equatorial Africa at that time. Although we speak casually of 'the Pygmies', they may be divided into three groups, namely the Mbuti, Twa and Mbenga. The differences between these ethnic groups of Pygmies is difficult for Europeans to identify. It has been speculated that their lack of height was caused by the forest environment in which they dwelt, in an analogous fashion to the phenomenon known as 'island dwarfism'. In the east and south of Africa lived the Khoi. They have the most ancient lineage of any human population in the world. They might be said to be the original humans. At the time of which we are speaking, they ranged over the whole of southern and eastern Africa. Although they were mostly, like the Pygmies, hunter-gatherers, the Khoi were on the cusp of pastoralism. This means that some of them were keeping herds of animals which moved with their owners in a similar way to the wandering Bedouin of the Sinai Peninsula, who roam the desert with their flocks of goats. The Khoi were very different in appearance to the Bantu. For one thing, their skin was much paler and for another their facial features had more in common with people living in East Asia than they do with the Bantu. Like most people from East Asia, the Khoi have an epicanthic eye-fold.

The Bantu practised slash and burn agriculture. They would chop down a section of forest and then burn the logs. All this would enrich the soil for a few years and so they would settle and plant yams. When the yields began to decline, they simply moved to a new part of the forest and repeated the process. In this way, they gradually expanded into the lands of both the Pygmies and the Khoi. The Pygmies and Khoi who resisted this encroachment upon their territory would have been at a huge disadvantage. Both groups were physically slighter than the Bantu, who were tall, healthy and strong, with a steady diet of nutritious food. As they colonized the continent, they killed, mated with or enslaved those with whom they came into contact. Today, the Bantu rule supreme in Africa and the Pygmies and Khoi live only in fragmented and geographically isolated pockets of land. The relevance of this account of ancient migration will be seen when we come to look at the situation relating to slavery in modern Africa.

It may be said that slavery in Africa existed from the earliest times; at least 4,000 years ago. Even to this day, the Bantu in countries such as the Democratic Republic of the Congo keep Pygmies as slaves, although this is not done in a harsh way. It is openly asserted that they regard the Pygmies almost as pets, a lingering relic of a situation dating back thousands of years before the birth of Christ.

Since there are no written records relating to the cultures of sub-Saharan Africa before the arrival of Arab explorers crossing the Sahara Desert in caravans of camels and the first voyages to that part of the world by sea undertaken by Portuguese traders, reconstructing the customs and way of life in Africa before the fifteenth century AD might seem a hopeless enterprise. There are though two methods by which we might build a picture of life there at that time. These may be broadly described as negative and positive evidence. Put together, they allow us to draw at least some conclusions about one or two features of the pre-literate societies of West Africa and at least one culture on the other side of the continent, which was to be found on the fringe of the Middle East.

What might be described as the negative evidence for the existence of slavery in Africa before the practice was actually recorded there is that we know that slavery existed across Europe, Asia, North Africa and North America from the earliest times. Whenever a structured society existed in ancient times, one with chiefs or kings and a social hierarchy, slavery in one form or another was present. In the Balkans and the Peloponnesian Peninsula, to give one example, only one nation did not hold with slavery. This was Macedonia and their rejection of this universal custom is so unusual that it is invariably the object of remark when the history of Macedonia is being discussed (Cotterell, 1980). From this perspective, it would have been remarkable if there had been no tradition of slavery in at least some parts of Africa before we find written references to it. There is though more definite evidence than this.

In 1938 a man called Isaiah Anozie was digging a cistern on his property in that part of Nigeria in which members of the Igbo tribe live. He unearthed some very fine bronze artefacts, which had been made using the *cere perdu* or 'lost wax' method of casting. He took these finds to the British administrative officer in the area and they were later sent to the Nigerian Museum. Although similar pieces had been found at Benin and Ife, this was the first time anything like them had turned up in that part of Nigeria. It was clear that something very interesting lay buried beneath the ground in that district.

Twenty years later, the archaeologist Thurstan Shaw was invited to carry out excavations where the bronzes had been found, which he did between 1959 and 1960. This archaeological expedition uncovered some more bronze items and also the tomb of an important individual who had been buried with great ceremony (Bahn, 1996). According to Shaw, his work was hampered by the somewhat backward and unsophisticated nature of the community in which he was working. He later wrote that;

> The Igbo–Ukwe excavation was far and away the most nerve-wracking excavation I have ever undertaken. This was partly because I very soon realised that I was onto something unique and important . . . in the night after the first bronze was discovered an attempt was made to steal it from under my bed. (Shaw, 1970)

Perhaps the most extraordinary discovery, and one which is relevant to the subject at which we are looking, was a burial chamber unearthed on the land of Isaiah Anozie's brother Richard. One man had been interred in a room built of wooden planks and then completely covered in earth. He wore a copper crown and was seated on a stool. In his hands had been placed a fly whisk and fan holder, perhaps symbols of office. Whoever he was, he must have been immensely rich and powerful, for the quantity of grave goods accompanying his burial was very great. In addition to many beautifully-made pieces of ceremonial bronzeware there were over 100,000 glass and carnelian beads. Carnelian is a semi-precious stone, much valued today by devotees of crystal healing. These beads had their origin in India and showed that there must have been extensive trading between those who lived in this part of West Africa and the ports on the Indian Ocean, thousands of miles away on the other side of Africa.

On the planks laid above the tomb of the person who was presumably a leader of the tribe, or perhaps the head of a religion, were found the remains of five people who had probably been sacrificed as part of the funerary rites. In many cultures across the world, it was the custom to kill slaves and bury them at the same time as a ruler, so that they could serve the dead man in the next life. The natural assumption is that these five individuals were part of this type of ceremony and this, by extension, suggests the existence of slavery at the time of the burial. Carbon dating has given the ninth century as the time when these five victims died, which predates European contact with that part of Africa by some 500 years. It has also been speculated that the presence of those many thousands of glass and carnelian beads, which were not made locally, indicates that they were obtained 'through trade for slaves, ivory, or spices' (Apley, 2001).

The fact that one man was given such a spectacular tomb indicates very strongly that the society to which he belonged was socially stratified to a high degree. In other words, there were very important men at the top of the social order and then various grades below them.

Once a society of this kind emerges from the loosely-knit and largely egalitarian bands of hunter-gatherers in early social structures, the existence of slavery may be more or less taken for granted. It was so in Europe and Asia and also both North and South America. This goes some way towards confirming that the bodies buried with the king or priest were those of slaves.

The tomb in Nigeria is not the only reason to suppose that slavery was customary in West Africa before Europeans became involved in the slave trade in that part of the world. There is also mention by Muslim writers of what was seen in sub-Saharan Africa in the fourteenth century. In 1351 a Berber scholar and explorer from Tangier set off across the Sahara from the Mediterranean coast of Morocco. Ibn Battuta had already travelled extensively in Asia and the Middle East and now he wished to see what lay south of his own homeland in the largely uncharted country of West Africa.

After crossing the Sahara in a camel caravan, Ibn Battuta arrived at Taghaza. This is now in the north of the modern-day country of Mali. Slabs of rock salt were mined here at the time that Ibn Battuta visited the town and the heavy work was undertaken by slaves from the Masufa tribe (Levtzion and Hopkins, 2000). After spending some time in Taghaza, the caravan moved south again, eventually reaching the capital of the empire of Mali, which lay on the banks of the River Niger. This was a Muslim realm, ruled by a black African sultan. Slaves were so common that Ibn Battuta was even given one as a present! After looking at other districts of West Africa, Ibn Battuta returned to Morocco, travelling with a caravan which was transporting 600 female slaves north across the Sahara (Defrémery and Sanguinetti, 1858).

To the east of Mali lay another black realm, which was so extensive at one time that it might not inaptly be called an empire. This was known as Kanem and our information about it comes principally from Arab geographers. In the seventh century, a leader of the Arab armies which conquered North Africa established a base in the middle of the dense forest which at that time covered part of the Tunisian coast. This grew into a city called Qairwan. Mosques and a university were founded and the city traded with a power which had grown up in Central Africa, not far from Lake Chad. Some of the nomadic tribes which roamed the savannah south of the Sahara Desert had banded together and put down roots, building walled towns. By the ninth century AD Kanem was one end of a busy route running south from Qairwan and ending in their own territory. Al–Yaqubi, a geographer writing at that time, said that, 'I have been informed that the kings of the blacks sell their own people without justification or in consequence of war' (Smith, 1972).

Kanem's prosperity was based upon exporting goods north to the Arab world of North Africa. Camel caravans travelled across the desert, carrying two principal cargos. One was salt; there were mines where this was dug out by slave labour. The other thing which was sold to the Arabs was people. Those who ran Kanem used to make regular raids into areas where the Bantu tribesmen were less well organized and then take them as prisoners to be sold to Arab merchants. In the early years of Kanem, about a thousand slaves a year were sold in this way, but by the fifteenth century, this had increased to 5,000 a year (Meredith, 2014). Both the internal economy of Kanem and its external mercantile activities were based upon slavery. Slaves worked the salt mines and also undertook much of the heavy and unpleasant physical labour in the cities and farms.

The centre of political power in Kanem shifted over the years and by the middle of the sixteenth century the realm was governed from Bornu, which lay on the banks of Lake Chad. Slavery was now very big business and it has been estimated that something in the region of two million slaves passed north over the centuries. All this great trade had nothing at all to do with Europe; it was centred around Tripoli, the capital of the modern state of Libya. Writing of the situation on the route taken by the slave caravans across the Sahara, Martin

Meredith, an expert in the history of this culture, had the following to say:

> Wells along the way were surrounded by the skeletons of thousands of slaves, mostly young women and girls, making a last desperate effort to reach water before dying of exhaustion once there. (Meredith, 2014)

By this time, after the fifteenth century, the realms of Kanem and then Bornu were Muslim, the people there having embraced Islam as a result of coming into so much contact with Arabs in the course of the slave trade. This meant of course that they were compelled to go further afield than their own lands in search of slaves to sell. Mindful of the prohibition laid down in the Hadith (the collected sayings of the Prophet Mohammed) about enslaving Muslims, they began raiding ever deeper into the forests of central Africa and bringing back prisoners of war who could be sold to the Arabs or forced to work in the salt mines. The slave-based economy of Bornu lasted, almost incredibly, until the nineteenth century and we shall look at the end of this traffic in helpless people as it existed at that time in a later chapter.

Enough has perhaps been said to show that slavery existed in sub-Saharan Africa at least as early as the ninth century and almost certainly earlier. It is necessary though to qualify this statement a little, because the word 'slavery' as it is commonly used today in the Western World allows little shade of meaning. It invariably refers to chattel slavery, that is to say the treating of humans like cattle; buying and selling them as though they were merely the property of their owner. Without doubt, some of the slaves in Africa were subjected to chattel slavery, but by no means all. Some slaves were genuinely seen as being members of the family. In at least one African culture, a slave could own slaves of his own. Elsewhere, slavery had more in common with the old European idea of serfdom, in which men and women were bound to a landlord's land, but could not be sold away from their homes. These various traditional ways of life continued into the colonial era and made the abolition of slavery a very complex proposition.

Nobody would deny that the interest of Europeans from the fifteenth century onward in buying slaves acted to encourage the slave trade in Africa, but they did not create it. Obviously, when new buyers appear on the scene of any commercial activity, especially those who are willing to buy as much of any given commodity as can be supplied, this is bound to stimulate the market. Demand has ever had the effect of increasing supply. Human nature being what it is, when it became known that the white visitors were desperate to acquire slaves, there were plenty of merchants only too ready to satisfy the demand. It has also been alleged that the European interest in the trade had the effect of altering the nature of slavery in Africa, but this is a complicated topic which will be discussed later.

It is perhaps possible to make the case that the demand for slaves in the Americas and also the insatiable appetite for them in the Middle East caused an unprecedented increase in the African slave trade, but one aspect of slavery can hardly be connected in any way with outsiders. This was the use of slaves across much of sub-Saharan Africa as victims of human sacrifice.

In many parts of the world, taking the lives of people for religious reasons or to ensure good fortune was simply an unremarkable part of the way of life. One very early record of human sacrifice undertaken as a way of securing a successful result in a chancy and uncertain enterprise is related in the Bible. We read in the Old Testament of Jephthah and the oath he swore. Chapter 11 of the Book of Judges tells how an Israelite leader called Jephthah was fighting against the Ammonite tribe and when things were looking uncertain, he sought to strike a bargain with God.

> And Jephthah vowed a vow unto the Lord, and said, if thou
> shalt without fail deliver the children of Ammon into mine

> hands. Then it shall be, that whatsoever cometh forth from
> the doors of my house To meet me, when I return in peace
> from the children of Ammon, shall surely be the Lord's, and
> I will offer it up for a burnt offering. (Judges 11:30, 31)

Unfortunately, it was Jephthah's daughter who emerged from his house as he returned from winning the battle and in due course, he sacrificed her as part of his bargain with the Lord.

In Europe, the remains of both animals and humans have been found buried in the foundations of buildings. This practice is known as 'foundation sacrifice' and it was widespread across Europe and Asia, as far east as Japan. It was particularly common in Celtic tradition (Ó Súilleabháin, 1945). This superstitious belief, that putting a human sacrifice in the foundations of a building will protect it from harm, is also found in the Bible. It is related in the Old Testament Book of Kings that when he was rebuilding Jericho, a local chieftain did this very thing;

> In his days did Hiel the Bethelite build Jericho: he laid the
> foundations thereof in Abiram his firstborn, and set up the
> gates thereof in his youngest son Segub (1 Kings, 16:34)

The gates of a city were popular places for such sacrifices, as were bridges and even ordinary homes. This practice was every bit as popular in Africa as it was in the rest of the ancient world and there are references to it in the writings of the first Europeans to visit Africa and record the customs which were observed there. The preferred victims of such sacrifices in Africa were usually slaves, some of whom had been acquired for the purpose (Brewster, 1971).

The Kingdom of Benin was in the south of what is now Nigeria and it was one of the places where European traders went when they wanted to buy slaves. Benin itself though, which included the kingdom of Dahomey, was already very familiar with slavery centuries before the first Europeans anchored off the coast. The trade in, and exploitation of, slaves had flourished in Benin long before the coming of white people to West Africa. Archaeological excavations have revealed, for instance, the sacrifice of slaves which was customary throughout most of the ancient world on the death of a king. We see this in so many cultures that it can hardly be expected that Africa would prove any exception. Archaeologist Graham Connah unearthed a total of forty-one female skeletons all buried in one pit. These dated from the thirteenth century and are assumed to be victims of human sacrifice; most likely they were slaves (Trigger, 2002).

So far, we have examined how slavery operated in West Africa. It is time now to consider an ancient kingdom on the other side of the continent, which is to say the region now occupied by the nation of Eritrea, which lies on the Red Sea. The first record of the kingdom of Aksum is from the early years of the Common Era.

Most studies of slavery in Africa seem to focus on West Africa to the exclusion of the rest of the continent, but the slave trade was thriving also on the coastal areas facing the Red Sea and Indian Ocean. Ethiopia, for instance, has a very long history of slavery, both indigenous and also practised by intruders from the Middle East. It is difficult sometimes to disentangle one from the other. Looking at the ancient kingdom of Aksum will illustrate this point.

Before we do so though, it might be instructive to enquire why we neglect to think of East Africa and its colonization by Arabs, but are very ready to consider the European influence on the other side of Africa. That we habitually refer to the transatlantic slave trade as *the* slave trade, a tendency remarked upon in the Introduction to this book, is one aspect of this unbalanced view of history.

Although the greater part of Africa had not advanced beyond the Stone Age by the time that European colonialists staked out their claims in the nineteenth century, there was one part of sub-Saharan Africa which boasted the remains of a great empire which had flourished thousands of years earlier. Whether this was a genuinely African civilization or one established by an earlier wave of colonization is an interesting point. At its height the kingdom of Aksum straddled the Red Sea, covering the whole of what is now the independent country of Eritrea, parts of Ethiopia, a large chunk of the Sudan and also much of Yemen in the Arabian Peninsula. We will deal with this particular case in Chapter 5, as it is of great importance when examining the origin and growth of that other slave trade which is so often neglected when looking at African history; that of the East African slave trade. We end this chapter with a look at the first European involvement in slavery in Africa, which took place at a time when the most important seafaring power was not Britain but its oldest ally, Portugal.

The fifteenth century was a time of European expansion, with the first ships sailing to both India and the Caribbean. There were rich prizes to be gained for the merchants who were daring enough to blaze a trail by being the first to bring back gold or human captives from far-off places. However, it was spices which initially precipitated what we now think of as the Age of Exploration.

Europe, unlike much of the rest of the world at that time, relied heavily upon meat as a basic staple foodstuff. The reason for this is simply a matter of geography. In much of Africa and Asia, the growing seasons are long and the climate warm. This means that it is easier to support a population through crops and fruit. In most of Europe though, especially in the fifteenth century when the continent was in the grip of what is sometimes known as the Little Ice Age, winter was long and summer short. Animals can be slaughtered in the autumn and their meat can be salted and preserved for long periods of time. It may become stale and tough if kept too long, but it remains edible and nutritious. However, chewing your way through such meat can be a little less than pleasurable and so the addition of spices had the potential to revolutionize mealtimes. The problem is that although in Europe we have herbs such as mint, thyme and so on, these are rather bland. Spices like pepper and cloves grow in hot countries and have to be imported.

Up to the end of the fifteenth century, all spices arrived in Europe after being carried overland from Asia. This made them expensive, for the merchants and traders only undertook the complicated and hazardous business of bringing goods thousands of miles across country that was harsh and sometimes hostile, if there was a good profit to be made from doing so. So high did this drive the prices of commodities brought to Europe in this way that there was, around the time that Columbus made his first voyage across the Atlantic Ocean, a saying in Europe; 'As dear as pepper' (Falkus, 1994). This was one of the main driving forces behind the expansion from Europe which took place at that time, the search to secure spices directly from those who grew them in India and other parts of south and East Asia. When Columbus set off across the Atlantic and Vasco de Gama sailed south around the Cape of Good Hope, they were not exploring the world and forging new sea routes for the sake of it; they were seeking new ways to India to obtain the spices which grew there.

This is, by the way, why there seem to be so many 'Indians' in the world. West Indians, North American Indians, Indians from South America, those actually from India and of course the people in the East Indies. When Columbus reached the Caribbean, he was searching for a route to India and assumed that he had reached a part of that country, which is why he called those living there 'Indians'.

It is fascinating to think that it was this desire for cheap pepper which led to the whole transatlantic slave trade. The discovery of the Americas was a by-product of this quest and so too was the acquisition by Europeans of slaves from West Africa. The sequence of events, although nobody at the time was thinking particularly of slavery, led inexorably to the exploitation of new territories for the purposes of mining and agriculture and a consequent need for unlimited numbers of labourers. Of course, when new lands came to light, as they did in 1492 when Columbus made landfall in the Caribbean, it was inevitable that he should bring back specimens of the natives whom he encountered there. This was something of a tradition and exactly the same thing had happened half a century earlier when the crew of a ship anchored off the coast of West Africa had thought it a good idea to take a few people back with them when they returned to Europe.

Africa was as interesting from the point of view of exploration and exploitation as the New World would later become. It was not that anybody specifically had in mind the idea of beginning the slave trade or anything of that kind, merely that ships which had reached distant shores needed to bring back evidence that such voyages could be profitable for those who backed them financially. It seemed to men like Columbus only natural that he should return from his trip across the Atlantic with a few natives and so too did another pioneer half a century earlier, who had sailed south rather than west.

When a young captain called Antam Goncalves set off from Portugal in 1442 he had a mundane commission from Prince Henry, who became known as the Navigator, to bring back seal skins and oils (Williams, 1970). Goncalves though saw a chance to make a name for himself by exceeding his instructions and returning with some human captives. He knew that the prince was keen to become involved in the business of spices and gold. The Arabs were making good money from this trade, as well as that in slaves which were still being brought across the Sahara from West Africa.

So it was that when he reached the coast of West Africa, Goncalves decided that in addition to the seal skins and oil, he would curry favour with Prince Henry by bringing him a few black people as well. He took his men ashore at night and they went in hunt of some natives who might be taken on board their ship. There was a fierce skirmish, in the course of which three Africans were killed, but eventually a few black people were indeed taken prisoner. One of these was a man called Adahu, who spoke Arabic. By good fortune, the expedition had a Portuguese interpreter on board who understood Arabic and it soon became clear that Adahu was prepared to help the sailors in acquiring as many slaves as they wanted. He explained that he was himself a leader, the equivalent perhaps of a minor prince or nobleman, and had access to the local traffic in slaves. Tempting as the offer was, it was decided to take those whom they had captured back to Portugal and let others make of Adahu's suggestion what they would.

Prince Henry was delighted to see that what had looked like a routine trading trip had found a source of exotic manpower which could be tapped. Antam Goncalves had correctly gauged the ruler's likely reaction and was rewarded accordingly. Henry was particularly enchanted with Adahu and gave him some splendid clothes to wear. He was also very interested to hear that some black Africans themselves were already operating a slave trade of their own which he might be able to exploit. He agreed that Adahu could be returned to his home and that the two of them would become allies in the export of slaves from Africa to Portugal.

We might stop for a moment and think about a common theme which we saw in slavery in other times and different parts of the world. This is the tendency to prefer slaves to belong to other cultures or ethnicities than one's own. The Bible of course sets out rules for slavery which carefully distinguish between Hebrew slaves owned by other Hebrews and foreigners who might have been taken as prisoners of war. In the Old Testament Book of Exodus, to give one example, there is a commandment that Hebrew slaves must be released after six years, in contrast to foreign slaves, who may be held in bond indefinitely (Everett, 1997). This is a recurring theme; we see precisely the same principle at work in the Code of Hammurabi and also in Muslim nations, where the enslavement of Muslims was prohibited. Between the years 642 and 708 AD, Arab armies conquered North Africa and enslaved many of the Berbers living there. Their religion though forbade them from making slaves of any professed Muslims whom they encountered (Pipes, 1981).

In sub-Saharan Africa, much the same principle was adhered to, that is to say that the majority of slaves were acquired through warfare. Prisoners of war became slaves and their daughters and wives often ended up as extra wives for important men in the conquering tribe.

In other words, black Africans were not merely the passive victims of slavery, which is the way in which they are almost invariably presented today, but some also took an active role in enslaving others and then selling them on to a third party. Arabs and Tuaregs may have been preying upon them and taking prisoners north across the Sahara Desert, but there was also a good deal of raiding between different ethnic groups of black Africans which usually ended up with one side carrying off slaves from the other. So it was that when Adahu assured Prince Henry that he would be able to arrange for a steady and reliable supply of black slaves for the Portuguese market, his words were not just an empty boast; he knew what he was talking about. Upon being allowed to go back to his own territory, Adahu was as good as his word and began supplying the Portuguese with as many black slaves as they required. Indeed, he and other African chiefs worked to such effect that over 10,000 slaves a year were being imported by Portugal at the height of the trade. By 1540, 10 per cent of the population of Lisbon consisted of enslaved Africans (Grant, 2009).

There can be no doubt that commercial interest in slaves by Europeans stimulated the African slave trade, but it certainly did not *create* it. Just as happened everywhere else throughout the course of recorded history up to that time, powerful rulers in sub-Saharan Africa were making slaves of their weaker neighbours and nobody saw anything in the least degree wrong with the custom. When some stroke of good fortune, such as the coming of Europeans eager to buy slaves, occurred, local leaders saw an opportunity to become prosperous and get hold of manufactured goods which had previously been unobtainable.

It is important that the establishment of the transatlantic slave trade, at whose early beginnings we have just looked, is not viewed as an enterprise in which all the advantage was on the side of the white Europeans, ruthlessly exploiting the simple-minded natives. Both sides were determined to cheat each other whenever the chance presented itself. It was not only slaves that the men from Portugal,

England, France and other countries hoped to take from Africa, but also gold. Not for nothing was the modern-day country of Ghana known until 1957 as the Gold Coast. The European traders for their part did their best to exchange faulty or broken muskets for the slaves which they wanted or to try and pass off cheap brassware as being valuable. The French explore Jean Barbot wrote that the Africans were similarly inclined to use sharp practices, saying that, 'the dexterity of the blacks in sophisticating their gold was scarce imaginable' (Barbot, 1999). This was done by means of mixing the gold dust which they sold to the white men with brass or copper filings.

This image, of unscrupulous black Africans cheating white slave traders and of African chiefs hunting for slaves to sell so that they could be transported across the Atlantic to the Americas, is not perhaps what springs readily to mind when the average person thinks about the slave trade. The reason is that such a perspective shows the Africans in just as bad a light as the white people and this does not accord at all with our modern ideas. Helpless black people being ruthlessly exploited by avaricious whites is one thing, but black kings setting out hard bargains which white traders had little choice but to abide by sounds somehow wrong.

We have seen how the Portuguese took advantage of the slavery which already existed in Africa when they arrived, but what form did this take? Was it indistinguishable from the chattel slavery which came to be the accepted system in America and the Caribbean or was there more to it than that? This is not an easy question to answer, because all the societies of sub-Saharan Africa at that time were pre-literate and so wholly lacking in any recorded history. We generally have only the observations of white travellers upon which to rely when looking into the slavery among black people which they encountered as soon as they arrived in Africa. This presents us with a slight difficulty, because of course we are all of us prone to create the world in our own image. Since the Portuguese were interested only in buying slaves and owning them as though they were so many domestic animals, it is hardly surprising that they assumed that the Africans with whom they dealt had a similar attitude to slaves. There, however, they were probably mistaken.

In Africa in historical times, that is to say after the arrival of European traders and colonists, it was seen over the years that some slaves belonging to wealthy people were actually attached to their masters almost as closely as though they had been members of their families (Miers and Kopytoff, 1977). Even if they technically had the authority to sell such family slaves, it would have been a grave breach of custom to do so. Instead, the slaves sold to the white men were those who had been taken prisoner during raids and who had been captured so far away that they might be viewed as foreigners. By tradition in all cultures, foreign slaves captured by force of arms were fair game to be sold to somebody else. We may judge from the ease with which the Portuguese were able to buy slaves at this time and also by the activities on the other side of Africa, facing the Indian Ocean, that slavery was a common and accepted practice in at least those parts of Africa of which we have any knowledge.

When we read sometimes of the Age of Exploration or something similarly high flown, we must always bear in mind that when explorers from Europe reached Africa or the Americas in the late fifteenth century, their motive was of course profit and trade, rather than simply extending understanding of the physical and geographical nature of the world. Those who financed such expeditions hoped for a monetary reward. This might come in the form of stealing a march on rival merchants by discovering a quicker route to India and China or perhaps by finding a hitherto unknown source of gold or new kinds of vegetables or spices. When Christopher Columbus set out on his first transatlantic voyage in 1492, he hoped of course to find a shortcut to the Far East, but found instead two new continents which contained much that would interest people in Europe.

Since the dawn of recorded history, gold has been seen as a most desirable commodity. Partly because of its rarity and also because

it never corrodes or loses its lustre, gold is the metal after which
everybody from the ancient Egyptians and Babylonians through to
present-day Russian oligarchs lusts. The nobility of medieval Europe
were similarly enamoured of gold and when it became known that
it was to be found in the Americas, there was great excitement. Of
course, there was in South and Central America a lot of jewellery and
other items made from gold which had already been produced. These
could be carried off by main force and taken to Europe, as was indeed
done. But mining gold requires a large labour force, because one has
to dig out at least two tons of rock in order to obtain a single ounce
of the precious metal. This means that a lot of work is entailed if the
enterprise is to be profitable. Since shipping hundreds of Europeans
over to the mines of Mexico or Peru would have required fleets of
ships and a fortune in wages for the imported workforce, a simpler
method suggested itself to the pioneers. Why not use those already
living in the area as labourers?

To begin with, nobody really thought in terms of slavery. It was
rather a matter of economic necessity. The native inhabitants of the
Americas showed themselves willing to work for decent remuneration,
but there was a problem. They were both very prone to falling ill
from diseases which had arrived from Europe and also did not appear
to have strong-enough constitutions to put in the long and arduous
shifts needed to extract enough gold from the mines to make the whole
thing profitable. Then too, if efforts were made to force them too hard
in their labours, the Indians could simply melt away and vanish to
another part of the country. This was, after all, their home territory.

The scale of the impact of European viruses and bacteria on the
New World is hard to comprehend today. The island of Hispaniola,
which is today divided between the countries of Haiti and Dominica,
provides a good illustration. In 1518, a little less than 30 years since
Columbus first reached that part of the world, Judge Alonso de Zuzao
wrote, 'When Hispaniola was discovered it contained 1,130,000
Indians; today their number does not exceed 11,000' (Saco, 1879).

This means that the population of the island had been reduced to a thousandth of what it had been before the arrival of Europeans. Other islands in the Caribbean were similarly decimated by disease and also the random massacres perpetrated upon them by explorers desperate to find any gold which had been concealed. In the first 50 years after the arrival of the Spanish, the population of Mexico declined by 90 per cent (Cooper, 2019).

Gold was certainly to be found in Mexico and South America, but the islands of the Caribbean possessed a natural resource which would prove to be even more lucrative in the long run than reefs of gold. This was their perfect climate for growing certain crops which were very expensive to buy in Europe and had to be imported from traders and merchants who charged as much as the market was worth for their goods. The most important of these was sugar.

From the earliest times, people have always found something peculiarly enticing about the taste of sweet things. In Europe and the Middle East, the sweetest thing known was honey and for thousands of years this was the epitome of sweetness. When the Lord offered to lead Moses and the Children of Israel to the Promised Land, it was only natural to refer to it as a land flowing with milk and honey; the idea that it contained the sweetest substance known to the ancient world automatically made the place sound attractive.

In India, there was a source of even greater sweetness than honey. This was sugar, which was extracted from the sugar cane plant, a type of grass which originated in New Guinea. The cultivation of sugar cane spread from New Guinea to China and India and it was in India that crystalline sugar was first produced (Snodgrass, 2004). From India both the plant, and the method of producing sugar from it, moved westwards to Persia and the Arab world. About a thousand years ago, the cultivation of sugar cane was introduced to Europe, by means of the Arabs who at that time occupied Spain. It began to be grown in the Canary Islands and on Columbus' second voyage across the Atlantic he took some sugar cane plants to Hispaniola, with a view to seeing if the climate there would be suitable for the commercial growing of sugar cane.

So used are we today to scattering sugar about with gay abandon, that it is difficult to understand that in sixteenth-century Europe it was a rare and costly spice, kept under lock and key in the homes of the rich and aristocratic. Because it was such a novelty, and the taste so delightful, sugar was sprinkled on meat and fish as often as on what we would today regard as more appropriate dishes like stewed fruit. The idea of being able to grow large quantities of such a precious crop was enough to precipitate something in the nature of a gold-rush in South America and the Caribbean. The only problem was that after the local population had been decimated, there were no workers who could engage in the cultivation of the crop.

It was the Portuguese who first thought of using African slaves to cultivate sugar on plantations in the New World. They had already experimented with plantations on the North Atlantic islands of Madeira and the Azores, but with limited success. It was rightly guessed that these locations were too temperate to provide optimum conditions for growing sugar cane (Curtin, 1999). Fortunately, an agreement reached with Spain in 1494 gave Portugal the ideal place for their sugar plantations. Because Portugal and Spain were both making voyages to hitherto unknown parts of the world and new territories were being opened up at the end of the fifteenth century with astonishing rapidity, there was a very real danger that the two nations would come into conflict. Therefore the Treaty of Tordesillas divided the world into spheres of influence. A line was drawn 1,185 miles to the west of the Cape Verde Islands, which lie off the coast of West Africa. Everything to the east of that line was to be open to the Portuguese, but west of it would be allocated to Spain. It was an act of supreme hubris on the part of the two Iberian nations that they felt able to divide up the whole world in this way, but there it was. A consequence was that Spain was able to claim much of South

America as being its exclusive property, other than Brazil, which would belong to Portugal.

The transatlantic slave trade began just 13 years after Columbus first reached the New World. The Spanish had been swift to follow the Portuguese in heading for the Americas and both countries did their best to force the natives whom they encountered to work in the mines and plantations which they set up. As we have seen though, the aboriginal inhabitants of the Americas fell prey to European diseases and were also prone to running off. If they were prevented from escaping, they often killed themselves. There was another difficulty with using Indians for agricultural work and that was that they did not have any real concept of a settled lifestyle. Many were hunter-gatherers, who did not cultivate land at all and simply relied upon catching enough animals and finding sufficient wild plants for their needs. Elsewhere, some followed a 'slash and burn' method of farming, moving on when the soil in one area was exhausted. To the Europeans, both these lifestyles were unfamiliar and strange; they were used to living rooted to one spot.

The people of West Africa, in contrast to the natives of the Caribbean and South America, were used to living in permanent settlements and tilling the earth to grow crops and this, together with their physical hardiness, made them appear a better prospect to the Spanish and Portuguese colonists than the feeble and feckless Indians. In 1505, a ship sailed from the Spanish port of Seville carrying seventeen Africans and a cargo of mining equipment to Central America. Eleven years later, the first shipload of sugar grown on a slave plantation in the Caribbean arrived in Spain. A decade later, the first shipment of slaves was taken directly from West Africa to the Caribbean. The transatlantic slave trade had begun.

West Africa was really a staging post for the Portuguese, as they continued their efforts to reach India by sea. In 1498, just a couple of years before the dawn of the sixteenth century, Vasco de Gama sailed

around the Cape of Good Hope and headed north into the Indian
Ocean. As he progressed along the coast of East Africa, he found that
his were not the only ships sailing these seas. What he encountered
as he reached as far north as what is now the East African country
of Tanzania, which includes the island of Zanzibar, was an extensive
network of maritime trade routes, linking together Africa, India and
the Far East. These shipping lanes were used by Arabs. Because they
were Muslim, the traders whom the Portuguese came across were
already in a sense their enemies, both for mercantile and doctrinal
reasons. They were not only enemies of Christ's church on earth,
they were blocking the advance of Portuguese trade and colonialism.
In Chapter 5 we shall see who these people were and how they were
connected with the slave trade in Africa. Before that though, we return
to North Africa and see what was happening there while Europeans
were making their first contact with sub-Saharan Africa.

Chapter 4

The Arab Slave Trade in North Africa from the Seventh to the Fifteenth Century

In the last chapter we saw that slavery was being practised in West Africa when Europeans first visited the area; it was not imported and imposed upon Africans, although there can be little doubt that slave trading increased dramatically once it was realized that the white people had a seemingly insatiable desire to acquire slaves to take overseas. This is one stimulus which slavery in Africa received. The other cause of an exponential growth in the capture, buying and selling of slaves in that part of the world was the arrival of the Arabs. Over 2,000 years ago Semites from the Arabian Peninsula colonized part of East Africa and established an empire there. This, the Kingdom of Axum, took part in the trade in and use of slaves and we shall look shortly be looking in some detail at this little-known culture.

Although they were later heavily involved in the slave trade in East Africa, the first major Arab influence on the trade began in that part of Africa which forms the southern shore of the Mediterranean Sea. We saw in an earlier chapter that the Egyptians, Romans, Greeks, Carthaginians and Garamantes had all been connected with slavery in North Africa, the coast which is today made up of the countries of Egypt, Libya, Tunisia, Algeria and Morocco. In the seventh century, the religion of Islam was founded by the Prophet Mohammed in and around the cities of Mecca and Medina, in what is now Saudi Arabia. Inspired by the teaching of Islam to carry its message from Arabia to the rest of the world, the Arabs invaded neighbouring countries and then swept across the Sinai Peninsula into Egypt and, from there, west towards the Atlantic. Part of this fervour was religious, but there was also a strong business end to the crusade, in that slaves could also be captured in large numbers. Slavery had always been an integral part of the way of life in the Arabian Peninsula and the founding of Islam seemed at first unlikely to affect this. After all, the Prophet himself owned slaves and so the practice could hardly be forbidden to his followers. It was only in later years, when all the sayings of Mohammed were collected together in the commentary known as the Hadith, that it was fully realized by all Muslims that the nature of slavery had to change.

Between the years 642 and 708 AD, the whole of North Africa fell to the Arab armies and about 300,000 of the Berbers living in the conquered areas were captured and became slaves (Pipes, 1981). The Arabs had no scruples at all about slavery and nor was it forbidden by the religion which they had lately adopted. Invading other nations and reducing them to slavery was what every other culture in the world tended to do when they went to war, but Islam now imposed a new restriction on the custom; one which was to have far-reaching and long-lasting consequences.

We pause at this point to consider the fact that working out the exact translation of a code of law written 1,500 years ago in another language can be a demanding and sometimes uncertain enterprise. This is especially so when it comes to the matter of slaves in this particular case, because several obscure euphemisms were used to refer to the subject. One of these was to refer to 'those whom the right hand possesses' and another was simply to use the Arabic word for 'property'. Such euphemisms can only be deciphered by examining the context of a passage from either the Hadith or Quran.

In the Hadith, which contains accounts of Mohammed's life and teachings, new ways of treating slaves are set out in detail. They are, for instance, to be regarded as fellow human beings and not mere objects or possessions. Freeing slaves is explicitly stated to be a meritorious act and one pleasing to God. Slaves could not be killed or otherwise mistreated. Nor could they be mutilated. This meant that castrating males for the purpose of creating eunuchs to guard a harem was now forbidden to devout Muslims. The Prophet said, 'Whoever kills his slave, we will kill him: whoever mutilates [his slave], we will mutilate him, and whoever castrates [his slave], we will castrate him' (Sunan an-Nasa'i 4736).

Perhaps the most radical change in perspective relating to slaves, and the one which was to have a disastrous effect upon both Europe and, a century or two later, East Africa, was that an absolute prohibition was laid upon the enslavement of Muslims. Previously, tribes in Arabia had had no compunction about raiding each other's territory and capturing people to either keep or sell as slaves, but with the ever-growing adoption of Islam, not only among the Arabs but also in other parts of Asia and along the coast of North Africa, getting hold of new slaves meant that the Arabs would need to cast their nets a little further. The only test of whether a person was a Muslim was a simple one. If somebody was able to declare, 'There is no God but Allah, and Mohammed is his messenger', then that was that. He was immune from being taken into slavery. This was not sufficient to bring about the release of anybody who was already a slave, although both the Qur'an and the Hadith made it plain that granting freedom to such a slave was a very desirable course of action. A good Muslim would only be able to own slaves who were non-Muslims and had been captured in battle or children born to a woman who was herself a slave.

For the next 700 years or so, the main source of slaves for the Arab world was Europe, and in particular Russia and other Slav lands. Indeed, for centuries 'slave' and 'Slav' were synonymous; the English word 'slave' is actually derived from 'Slav'. Vikings made raids into Russia and captured as many Slavs as they could and then took them south to sell to the Arabs. Nor did the Vikings limit themselves to out-of-the-way places like Russia. When nobody opposed them, they were quite prepared to sweep through parts of what is now Germany, seizing people to take and sell in the slave markets of the Middle East and North Africa. Writing in the eighth century, Paul the Deacon described, 'innumerable troops of captives' being taken south in this way from Europe (Foulke, 1974).

For the first few centuries after the rise of Islam, most of this trade in European slaves had little effect on Africa. The religious authority in the Muslim world, known as the Caliphate, moved between Mecca, Damascus and Baghdad. It was when the centre of gravity settled in what is now the Turkish city of Istanbul, but was at that time called first Byzantium and then Constantinople, that North Africa became an important location for the slave trade. It also became the launching point for raids on Europe aimed at capturing slaves. All this coincided with the rise of the Ottoman Empire, the centre of which was the territory we know today as Turkey.

From 1517, the Caliphate was firmly established in Istanbul where it remained until the twentieth century. The various parts of North Africa such as Tripoli and Tunis were nominally provinces of the Ottoman Empire and those living there realized that there was a very profitable market in supplying the empire with slaves. There were two possible ways of getting hold of slaves. There was the old way of sending caravans south across the Sahara and collecting black prisoners. This was how the Carthaginians and Egyptians had always done things. However, being maritime nations, the Moroccans, Tunisians, Algerians and Libyans had many fast ships and no shortage of daring sailors and adventurers who were only too happy to run a few risks if it meant the chance of making a fortune. So it was that instead of trekking across the barren wastes of the desert which lay on the fringes of their dominions, some merchants financed expeditions to seize slaves from the coastal districts of Europe.

Perhaps readers are wondering why the Ottoman Empire had such a desire for slaves. After all, there were no plantations of sugar cane or cotton to be cultivated in the Middle East, as was the case in the Caribbean and southern parts of North America. To begin with three types of slaves were in great demand. These were attractive young women, healthy and intelligent adolescent boys, and eunuchs. Apart from these categories, there was also a requirement for general labourers to undertake dirty, arduous and unpleasant work which was beneath the dignity of Muslims.

There is something quaint about the word 'concubine' and it is possible that modern readers may not be altogether sure as to what a concubine actually was. Essentially, a concubine is a woman who has a regular sexual relationship with a man, despite not being married to him. The status of concubines varied enormously, not only in the Muslim world but at other times and places too. Some concubines have been little more than sex-slaves or mistresses, but others have been accepted as being almost on the level of wives. Concubines are a by-product of polygamy and of course this was a practice not forbidden by either Islam or the Bible. Having a large number of wives and concubines was a sign of wealth and importance in the Muslim world for many centuries, although even the most famous of sultans never matched King Solomon, of whom it was written that he had 700 wives and 300 concubines (1 Kings 11:3).

Although black African women were taken as concubines, the preference was for women with lighter skin; the lighter the better. In fact, if white European women could not be obtained then any Africans had to be as light-skinned as possible and those with straight noses were preferred to those of a more typically African appearance. Illustration 7 is of light-skinned young women from what is now Ethiopia being captured by slave traders and taken north to the harems of the Ottoman Empire. Because of this, women from Ethiopia and Somalia were more in demand than those from central Africa. The reason for this was that in these areas, Arabs had already been having dealings for many centuries and they had left their mark in the form of babies sired with black women. Over the years, this had led to Ethiopians being a good deal more light-skinned that those to the south or west of their country. It must be remembered that Ethiopia is only separated from the Arabian Peninsula by less than 20 miles of sea and that Semites had been visiting and trading in the area since Biblical times.

Those with enough power and money to have many wives and concubines kept them in special quarters called a harem and, for the most obvious reasons, wished to ensure that the guards of such places were unable to engage in illicit sexual relations with the women. The solution was a simple, if brutal. Men who were to be involved in the running of, or who even came into close contact with, the harem were castrated. Because Muslims were forbidden by their religion from castrating slaves, they were obliged to acquire men who had already been castrated and this gave rise to a thriving industry in Southern Europe, where Slavs who had been enslaved were taken and their penises and testicles removed. If they survived this process, for the mortality rate from such crude surgery was extremely high, the victims would then be sold to the Ottoman Empire.

The last of the three categories of highly-desired slaves were boys who could be trained to hold important positions in the households of important men or as members of the civil service which ran the Caliphate. There were advantages to having foreigners employed in such posts, because without family connections among the Muslims and lacking any particular religious or political allegiance, such men would be less likely to become involved in plots or intrigues, something which was very common in the Arab and later Ottoman courts.

Because provinces like Tunis were so far from whatever Caliphate happened to be in power, they were able to behave with a degree of autonomy, always providing of course that they did not openly rebel and formally acknowledged the authority of the Caliph in Istanbul. What this meant in practice was that the slavers of the Barbary Coast, which is what North Africa was known as at that time, were able to keep most of their profits themselves, as long as they handed over a certain percentage of their catch to the ruler who was looking after the province for the Caliphate. This meant that on returning from a slave-raiding expedition, the slavers typically handed over an eighth of their captives to the ruler of whichever port they had set out from.

It will be observed from what has been said above that white slaves of European origin were just as likely to be found in North Africa as were black people brought north from sub-Saharan Africa. Without reliable information and statistics from censuses and so on, it is impossible even to hazard a guess as to which ethnicity was the most common among slaves in North Africa at that time. Looking at the modern Arabs of North Africa, it is not at all uncommon to find blue eyes or fair or ginger hair, an infallible indicator of European heritage. Encountering Arabs in that part of the world whose ancestry is noticeably African is not as common, except in Egypt. There may be two reasons for this, the first and most obvious being that many of the guards in harems were, at least in the later centuries following the rise of Islam, Africans, and they these unfortunate men were invariably castrated. This would automatically ensure that they would not contribute to the gene pool which we see today. In the second place, it was in some harems routine for mixed-race babies of obviously African appearance to be simply killed. Infanticide was not as frowned upon as is the case in the modern world.

Black African slaves may well have made up a large proportion of eunuchs in the harems of wealthy and powerful Muslims in later centuries, but until the fifteenth century, it was far more likely to find white eunuchs. This trade, which introduced eunuchs and other white slaves in North Africa for 500–600 years, has more or less faded from our consciousness. This is most probably a by-product of the mindset at which we have looked, which regards the transportation of black Africans across the Atlantic as *the* slave trade.

It must be remarked that although the castration of slaves in the Caribbean or America did take place from time to time, it was a very rare event, usually inflicted as a means of punishment or retribution. It was not routinely carried out for the simple reason that most men subjected to this process died of blood loss or subsequent infection. In short, it was usually tantamount to a death sentence and the consequent loss of a valuable piece of 'property'. The North African market for castrated males, on the other hand, was extensive and so great care was devised in mitigating the effects of this terrible operation.

We have seen the Hadith specifically forbids Muslims from castrating slaves, but there was no prohibition on acquiring one who had already been treated in this way and this gave rise to what was in effect an industry in southern Europe which was devoted to supplying castrati to North Africa. Once they arrived at Tunis, Tripoli or Algiers, they were then sold on to other parts of the Muslim world. Since readers are unlikely to have heard about this, it might be helpful to give a little background information; both about the trade in slaves to North Africa and also the methods used for castration.

The Slav people had their origin in Western Russia and over the years spread from there into Ukraine and the Balkans and as far south as Greece. Just as there was a prohibition in Islam on the taking of Muslims as slaves, so too did the Catholic Church frown upon those dealing in Christian slaves. Because they were heathens, being neither Muslim nor Christian, the Slavs were acceptable merchandise in both Europe and Africa. The same applied to the German tribes, who also worshipped pagan gods. The Vikings were therefore able to capture Germans and Slavs and either sell them directly to Muslims or to European middlemen who would turn some of them into eunuchs, thus greatly increasing their value. It was big business.

The young male slaves who were not immediately exported to the Barbary States often ended up in Venice or the French city of Verdun, where specialized 'castration houses' existed (Tracy, 2013). It was here that the production of eunuchs was undertaken for the Muslim market. The first thing to understand about the creation of eunuchs is that the mortality rate for men who were castrated at that time was exceedingly high; one estimate puts it at 90 per cent. Many of those treated in this way bled to death, others died of infection and some whose wounds had been cauterized to prevent infection died of ruptured bladders because scar tissue formed in the urethra, making it impossible to void urine. Even under ideal circumstances, the number of deaths was still extremely high. In the sixteenth century a Coptic monastery in Egypt was renowned for producing eunuchs and had the operation and aftercare down to a fine art. Even so, despite taking every precaution and being very skilled, two-thirds of those castrated there died (Wilson and Roerhrborn, 1999). This was under the optimum conditions for the time.

It had been found that death was more likely to occur in grown men than in pre-pubertal boys and so these were the preferred victims. The only form of castration acceptable in the Muslim world for those who would be guarding harems was the complete excision of both testicles and penis. Once this had been done, the wound was cauterized with a red-hot iron, to prevent excessive blood loss. It also had as a side effect the prevention of infection. The problem with this technique though was that scar tissue forming in the urethra would prevent the bladder from draining. If this happened, then the bladder would simply burst like a balloon, which was invariably fatal. If the boy was unable to urinate three days after the operation, then 'the passages have become swollen and nothing can save him' (Penzer, 2005). Death was certain.

In the European castration houses an ingenious means was devised to reduce the danger of death from a ruptured bladder. Immediately the penis had been removed and a hot iron used to staunch the bleeding, a small metal plug was inserted into the urethra. For three days, the boy was not allowed to drink or urinate. If on the third day, urine flowed freely when the plug was removed, then the operation had been a success. For the rest of his life, the eunuch would be obliged to sit or squat in order to urinate. Incontinence was a frequent problem and for many the plug became a permanent feature of life. Many of these unfortunate souls suffered leakage and it was not uncommon for eunuchs to smell of urine. Once a eunuch had been created in this way, the value of the slave soared. Of course, if he died as a result of this barbarous process, then the price paid for the slave would be altogether lost and so the slavers who invested in this business had a very strong incentive to make the operations as successful as possible.

Once the men and boys had recovered from the mutilation to which they had been subjected, they could be transported to the Muslim world. This was usually done by the simplest and most direct route, which was by ship from Venice to one or other of the Barbary States. This shipping of slaves to North Africa was often a two-way process. Once the eunuchs had been delivered, the slavers would often collect other slaves, usually black Africans, and take them to back to Venice (Falkus, 1994). There was in much of Europe a desire to have black manservants as novelty items. Then too, the galleys of Venice and other European powers required slaves as their motive force.

One curious point about the trade in slaves between North Africa and Europe is that much of it was in the hands of a mysterious guild of whom few people have ever heard. It is sometimes asserted today that the transatlantic slave trade was, in the eighteenth century, dominated by Jews. This is open to question, but no such uncertainty attaches to the role of Jews in the medieval slave trade involving the export of white slaves to North Africa. It is easy enough to see why this should have been.

For perhaps a thousand years, Christian Europe was locked in combat with the Muslim world of North Africa and the Middle East. At times, the Muslims appeared to have the upper hand, sweeping up into Spain and setting up a Caliphate there and even crossing the Pyrenees into France. At other times, the Christians invaded and conquered the Middle East, establishing a kingdom in Jerusalem. Centuries later, Muslim armies advanced to the very gates of Vienna. By reason of this continuous hostility, Muslim merchants trading in Europe or Christian slave traders in North Africa would both have been viewed with suspicion and mistrust. Jewish traders though, not being bound to either side in the clash of civilizations, were able to move through Europe, Africa and the Levant with relative ease. A guild of Jewish traders emerged, called the Radhanites. There is considerable debate about the origins of this body, although they are mentioned by both Arab and Christian writers in the Middle Ages as being involved in the slave trade.

Writing in the ninth century AD, an Arab called Ibn Khordadbeh gave a precise and detailed account of the various routes used by those trafficking in slaves. As Director of Posts and Police for a province of the Abbasid Caliphate, Ibn Khordadbeh was in the best possible position to know about such matters and his work, *The Book of Roads and Kingdoms*, is consequently regarded as being authoritative (Meynard, 1865). He was familiar with the Radhanites and wrote of them as being the people chiefly concerned with the importation of luxury goods into North Africa and the Middle East, specifically mentioning eunuchs.

> These merchants speak Arabic, Persian, Roman, Frankish, Spanish and Slav languages. They journey from West to East, from East to West, partly on land, partly by sea. They transport from the West eunuchs, female slaves, boys, brocades, castor, marten and other furs, and swords. (Meynard, 1865)

It will already have been seen that slavery and the slave trade in Africa is immensely more complicated that one at first supposes. The simple idea of slavery as entailing the capture and exploitation of black people by white has had to be abandoned and a much richer and more complex picture has emerged; one in which Europeans and Arabs, Jews, Muslims and Christians are all working to find the arrangement which most benefits their own financial position. It was said above that for the harems of Arabs and Ottoman Turks either European women or African women with European features were in demand. These latter were brought up into North Africa and the Levant via long established routes stretching from what is now the coast of Kenya, all the way to the Mediterranean coast of Egypt. It is at the origin of that particular part of the African slave trade that we shall now look.

Chapter 5

The Slave Trade in East Africa up to the Seventeenth Century

Fully to understand the East African slave trade, which was a ghastly business, rivalling in extent the far better-known transatlantic slave trade, we need to go back 2,000 years and see what was going on in those parts of the world where today we find the countries of Yemen, Ethiopia and Eritrea. Before doing so, perhaps it would be helpful to pause for a moment and consider how arbitrary is our division of the world into continents and the way that history often takes no heed of such modern geographical definitions.

The title of this book suggests that it should treat exclusively of slavery in Africa, but it is of course impossible to do so without discussing the reasons that some people there were captured and enslaved, and then thinking about their ultimate fate. This is certainly the case with the transatlantic slave trade, during which people in West Africa were initially enslaved by others from the same part of the continent but often for the purpose of selling them on to traders who would carry them off thousands of miles to another continent. Precisely similar considerations arise when we examine the history of slavery and the slave trade in East Africa. Africa is of course not an island, but is rather connected to Asia by a land-bridge known as the Sinai Peninsula. This means that the peoples and empires of Egypt, Rome and Greece, to give three examples, did not think of Africa as being a separate part of the world from Asia, for their cultures spanned both Egypt, which is in Africa, and also Israel, which is by modern ideas in Asia. This same situation existed also from the earliest times in the Horn of Africa.

The Horn of Africa is an African peninsula which juts out into the Gulf of Aden. It runs along the southern part of the Red Sea and Gulf of Aden and is the easternmost part of Africa. Ethiopia, Eritrea and Somalia now make up the Horn of Africa. At its narrowest, the point where the Red Sea becomes the Gulf of Aden, known as the Bab al-Mandab strait, just 18 miles separates Africa from Asia. It is hardly surprising therefore that this close proximity should have resulted in a trade route springing up between mainland Africa and Arabia, just as such routes did across the Sinai Peninsula. This area also formed part of a southern sea route to India and the Far East which was analogous to the more famous Silk Road along which Marco Polo travelled. This way across the Indian Ocean is sometimes known as the southern spice route. Various goods were exported from Africa in this way to India and beyond. These included ivory, incense, gold, exotic animals and of course slaves (Finkleman and Miller, 1998). In return, spices, ceramics and silk, among other things, were brought back to Africa.

It will not have escaped notice that the method of trading which we are describing here is indistinguishable from that which later became known as the Triangular Trade. The essential point about this system was that at no time were ships making pointless journeys; travelling empty-handed as one might not inaptly put it. In the Triangular Trade with which we are all familiar, slaves were carried from Africa to the Caribbean or America. From there, raw materials such as sugar, tobacco or cotton were taken to England and then a cargo of manufactured goods was taken to West Africa, where the whole process began again. This is a marvellously efficient and profitable way of going about things. It is exactly how the East African slave trade across the Indian Ocean worked, with all the ships being fully laden in whichever direction they were travelling.

It has been claimed that the Horn of Africa was a centre for the trade in slaves as early as 1400 BC (Pankhurst, 1968). The evidence for this is scanty and sparse, but there can be no doubt that 2,000 years ago a flourishing trade in slaves was operating in this part of Africa. This centred around the Kingdom of Axum, which is sometimes spelled 'Aksum'. Axum was an African and Arabian culture which existed for almost 1,000 years in what are now Ethiopia, Eritrea and Yemen.

Very little is known of the people known as the Sabaeans, who lived in the south of Arabia. It is sometimes suggested that their country, Saba, is the Sheba mentioned in the Bible, whose queen visited King Solomon. The story of the Queen of Sheba is told briefly in two books of the Bible, namely the First Book of Kings and the Second Book of Chronicles. It is worth recounting here for the light which it might shed upon one of the oldest kingdoms in Africa, that of Ethiopia. According to Scripture,

> And when the queen of Sheba heard of the fame of Solomon concerning the name of the Lord, she came to prove him with hard questions. And she came to Jerusalem with a very great train, with camels that bare spices, and very much gold, and precious stones. (2 Chronicles 9:1)

The two monarchs must have hit it off, because when she returned to her own country, 'King Solomon gave unto the queen of Sheba all her desire, whatsoever she asked, beside that which Solomon gave her of his royal bounty'. The only clue about the whereabouts of Sheba is that in Matthew's Gospel Jesus refers to her as 'the queen of the south'.

If Sheba was a historical kingdom and this story is not merely a fantasy like the tales of the *Arabian Nights*, then it is a reasonable assumption that the kingdom lay somewhere in the Arabian Peninsula. This seems likely when we read about another episode which is related as taking place during Solomon's reign. The Phoenicians, of whom mention has already been made in connection with their colonization of the Mediterranean, were the most able and proficient sailors of that time, around 1000 BC. It has been suggested that they visited Cornwall to buy tin and there is also some reason to suppose that they circumnavigated Africa. They were certainly useful to King Solomon, who struck a deal with King Hiram, who ruled Phoenicia. In exchange for some territory in the north of his kingdom, Solomon secured the right to cut down trees in Hiram's country and use the timber for projects in Israel. Of interest to the subject which we are examining in this book is the arrangement which Solomon made for providing the Phoenicians with access to the Red Sea and consequently the coast of East Africa. This was conditional on the sharing of technology relating to smelting. Both parties benefited enormously.

The Bible tells us that the Phoenician ships which sailed south from what is now the Israeli holiday resort of Eilat were absent for three years at a stretch and when they returned they carried cargoes of exotic animals, gold, silver and, most significantly, ivory (Mantoux, 1977). That ivory was brought back to the Middle East tells us at once that these ships had made the journey to Africa. That they had returned with precious metal also suggests that they had been visiting what would later come to be known as the Swahili Coast, that part of East Africa which faces the Indian Ocean. With whom were these adventurous sailors actually trading? They were after all merchants and not warriors: whatever they acquired must surely have been obtained peacefully, rather than simply being snatched from the owners. Would there not have been an insuperable difficulty as regards language if they bartered directly with the tribes living on the African coast?

It is to be hoped that readers will not be growing restless by this time and asking themselves what any of this ancient history has to do with slavery and the slave trade. We are about to make the acquaintance of an African kingdom whose connection with the slave trade lingered on until after the Second World War and has links with such well-known events in British history as the death of Gordon of Khartoum.

Returning for a moment to the subject of Sheba and its legendary queen, we note that there are any number of old legends which link the Queen of Sheba, King Solomon and what are now the countries of Ethiopia and Eritrea. Haile Selassie, the last emperor of Ethiopia, who was deposed in a military coup in 1974, claimed direct descent from the marriage between King Solomon and the Queen of Sheba. This legend has been circulating for at least a thousand years and probably two or three times as long. The emperors of Ethiopia claimed that their authority was founded upon this event. It is not only in the Bible that the Queen of Sheba is mentioned. She appears too in certain Muslim traditions and according to these old stories, Solomon did indeed marry this enigmatic woman. The Ethiopians say that their son then returned to his mother's kingdom and claimed the throne there. This kingdom covered not only much of what is now Yemen, but also a large chunk of East Africa. Readers may be asking themselves what grounds we have for giving credence to these old tales.

Centuries before the birth of Mohammed an Arab people known as the Sabaeans had established what might be said to amount to a colony in Africa. We have no direct historical evidence for this. All we know is that a kingdom existed which was partly in Arabia and partly in Africa. Some people today believe that this was a purely African state which crossed the Red Sea and colonized the south coast of Arabia, but there is good reason to suppose that it was actually the other way around and that it was the Sabaeans who went to Africa and imposed their rule there. After all, in the usual way of things, it is the language of the colonizer which enjoys the higher status in any colony. Those who were living in the area before it was colonized are obliged to learn to speak whatever language the invaders speak. So it is that in India today English is a language which all educated people speak and read. The number of people belonging to the colonial administration of India who took the trouble to learn Hindi or Gujarati was not great. In the same way, in those countries today which once formed part of the Axumite realm, it is Semitic languages such as Amharic, Tigrinya and Arabic which are spoken by those who feel themselves to be educated and cultured people. An African language called Oromo is also spoken by people in Ethiopia, but there is no reason to suppose that it was ever spoken in Yemen, which is where the homeland of the Sabaeans was. This suggests that it was the Sabaeans who went to Africa and imposed their language upon the inhabitants, rather than Africans who went to Arabia and expected people to learn Oromo.

Whoever founded the kingdom of Axum, it had by the second or third century AD grown to be a mighty power. One Persian writing in the third century said that Axum was one of the four great powers of the day, the others being Rome, China and Persia itself. The prosperity of Axum was founded, like that of Phoenicia and its colonies, on trade. Ships sailed from Yemen and the coast of Africa and carried slaves and ivory to India and China. They returned with cargoes of spices, such as cinnamon from what is now Sri Lanka, and also such luxuries as porcelain and silk from China. The advantage of this maritime route was that it avoided travelling thousands of miles through mountainous territory in Asia, passing through countries where tolls might have to be paid or bandits would be likely to attack a caravan.

There was nothing in the least remarkable about the export of slaves from Axum. Slavery was, after all, common enough through the whole of Africa and raiding neighbouring territories for slaves was part of the backdrop to life in Africa at that time. Axum is noted for its monumental architecture, buildings and obelisks of stone, and for the ruling class of the kingdom using slaves for the hardest physical labour would have seemed the most natural thing in the world. We talk today with horror of the concept of 'chattel slavery', treating humans like domestic animals, but that is merely our modern sensibilities at play. In Axum, as in almost every other part of the world at that time, selling slaves for profit was simply what was done.

This would all be in keeping with what we have so far learned about the institution of slavery, which is that outsiders or foreigners are invariably preferred for this purpose than fellow countrymen. If ancient Axum was an essentially Semitic or Arab nation or colony, then those black people outside its territory would have been seen as perfect candidates for enslavement. It might be remarked at this point that although it is not strictly speaking scientific evidence, it is none the less an undeniable fact that black people from this part of Africa look very different from the purer Bantus who live in West Africa. Set a Nigerian Igbo side by side with somebody from Eritrea or Sudan and the difference is immediately apparent. Ethiopians and those whose family origins lie near to the coast in this part of east Africa tend to have thinner noses, higher foreheads and lighter skins than is usual in much of Africa. In other words, they often look more like Arabs than they do Africans. It was this tendency towards light skins which made Ethiopian women so popular as concubines in the Ottoman Empire. Typically, African-looking women would more usually be employed as domestic servants, but the fine-featured and light-skinned Ethiopian women were sought after for the harem.

At the same time that slaves were being loaded onto ships and taken to India and China, others were being taken either by land or sea north towards Egypt. The Romans and the Ptolemies, the Greek dynasty which for a while controlled Egypt, both required slaves and the merchants of Axum were happy to supply their needs. These slaves were Africans who were captured in raids on inland districts.

The reason that the slave trade flourished particularly in Axum was that the place was not overly endowed with natural resources. The one thing which that part of the world does have though is plenty of people. So it was that slavery was a natural commercial business in which to engage. For 300–400 years, Axum did well and the kingdom became wealthy from the slave trade. It began to decline in the late seventh century, with the rise of Islam and the unification of Arabia under the banner of the Prophet Mohammed. Yemen became part of the Muslim Arab world and the remnants of Axum in Ethiopia were left to go their own way.

Returning briefly to the matter of the Phoenician ships which travelled south from Israel, it would not be at all surprising if they had dealings with the Sabaeans. There would, after all, be many similarities between the Phoenicians and these Arabs; not least in the languages spoken. Even to this day, thousands of years later, there are enough similarities between Tigrinya, the language spoken in Eritrea, and the

Hebrew spoken in modern Israel to make some parts of the languages mutually intelligible. Common constructions such as 'Beit' for 'house of', is one such common ground. Christians in Europe and America are of course familiar with the town Bethlehem as the birthplace of Jesus. This is an anglicized version of the Hebrew name of the place, Beit Lechem, which translates as 'House of Bread'.

In 2019 news emerged of an archaeological excavation on the border between Ethiopia and Eritrea, during the course of which an ancient church dating back to the fourth century AD was uncovered. The site was called Bet Samati (CNN, 2019). Although this is name is Tigrayan, it is immediately recognizable to any speaker of Hebrew or Arabic as being made up of two phrases; 'House of' and 'I heard'. In Hebrew, 'I heard' is 'Shomati'. If the similarities between the languages of Eritrea and Israel are so close today, it is not difficult to imagine that they would have been even closer 2,000 or 3,000 years ago.

It was perhaps inevitable that with the rise of Islam, which is essentially a proselytizing religion, the days of Axum should be numbered. In Axum, Christianity was the chief religion, although some people in Yemen, including one of the rulers there, embraced Judaism. Other religions were of course anathema to the followers of the Prophet. Wherever they went, it was accepted that one either became a Muslim or ended up being killed or enslaved. This is in the nature of religious crusades, which is what the Arab expansion from their desert kingdom amounted to. The tradition of slavery which had grown so powerfully during that time lingered on and even as late as the twentieth century, that part of Africa was famed for its slave trade, of which more in a later chapter.

We have seen that one ancient culture in sub-Saharan African, that of the Axum Empire, was heavily influenced or even founded by Semites from Arabia. Like other civilizations of the time, Axum traded in slaves. Traders and explorers from the Arabian Peninsula were also active much further south; perhaps even as early as they were in Axum. On the coast of East Africa which is today part of

Kenya and Tanzania, the clues are very clear to see. After all, the capital of Tanzania is Dar es Salaam, a name with obvious Arabic origins. The chief language spoken in that part of Africa is Swahili, the most widely spoken indigenous language in the whole of Africa. Swahili was known colloquially at one time as 'Coast Arabic', because of the large number of Arabic expressions and loan words which it contains. The very name of the language is derived from the Arabic word 'sawahil', which means 'coast' (Dalby, 1998).

Two things brought Arabs this far south from their homeland; ivory and slaves. These two valuable commodities went together and the trade in one stimulated the other as a matter of course. Ivory is obtained from the tusks of elephants, although the horn of the narwhal and tusks of the walrus also yield this useful substance. From the earliest recorded history, ivory has been a byword for luxury. King Solomon decorated his palace with ivory and the Bible tells us the source;

> For the king had at sea the ships of Tarshish with the ships of Hiram: once every three years the ships of Tarshish came bringing gold and silver, ivory and apes and peacocks. (1 Kings 10:22)

That apes were included in the list of goods brought up the Red Sea to Israel hints strongly that at least some of the cargo had been acquired from Africa.

Ivory could be carved into ornaments, used for jewellery and combs, inlaid into wood to decorate furniture and for a hundred other things. We take plastic so much for granted that perhaps we seldom stop to ask ourselves what the Victorians would have used for piano keys or billiard balls. For thousands of years, ivory was seen as one of the most versatile materials in the world, which of course accounts for the fact that elephants have in the past been hunted almost to extinction.

There was one slight difficulty in collecting ivory and that was that elephant tusks are very large and heavy. The average tusk is something over 2m in length and weighs 23–45kg (51–99lbs). Once the Arab traders had landed on the coast of East Africa and then travelled many miles into the interior of the continent until they came across the elephants, how on earth were they to transport such weighty items as their tusks back to their ships? The answer to this problem was brilliant. If Africans could be captured and made into slaves, then they could carry the tusks, if necessary hundreds of miles, back to where the ships lay waiting. Instead of just ivory, the Arabs now had two useful things to sell when they returned to their homeland. The quest for ivory in East Africa thus became closely linked with the acquisition of slaves. Not only was this a way of avoiding the ruinously high costs which using hired labour would have entailed, it effectively doubled the profit for each expedition.

Long before Europeans began exploiting West Africa for slaves, the coast on the other side of the continent was the exclusive province of Arab slavers. They built ports and started settlements there, from which they exported ivory and slaves to North Africa and the Arabian Peninsula. For the Axumites, the chief focus of trade had been to the east; for the Arabs, it was north into their own lands. It is by no means impossible that it was the Sabaeans who influenced the Arabs to look to Africa as a source of slaves. Perhaps it is no coincidence that Yemen, the original home of the Sabaeans, is next to Oman. It was Oman which later came to dominate Zanzibar and the coast of East Africa.

Arab influence on what is sometimes called the Swahili Coast of Kenya and Mozambique dates back well over 1,000 years. There is evidence of Arab architectural design in the style of buildings from about the eighth century onward (Fleischer *et al*, 2015). This was of course the time when the Arabs were expanding at breakneck speed from their traditional homeland and forging their way across North Africa and into Europe, and also into the Middle East and Persia. It is hardly surprising that their influence should also have begun to stretch south as well.

There is no reason to think that the Arab presence in Zanzibar and the African coast was anything in the nature of a conquest or attempted colonization. When the Arabs began moving along the coast of North Africa, it was a quest for new territory and a desire to spread the word of Islam. Nothing of the kind happened on the east coast. In all probability, it was purely a series of commercial ventures which brought them to that part of the world. Once they had begun dealing with various places though, it was only natural that they should then begin to engage in the slave trade. As we have seen, there was an inexhaustible demand for slaves in the Arab world and there were also maritime trade routes to the east which were still in use. The legacy of the slave trading of the Swahili Coast lingers on to this day in south Asia, although these traces are unknown to most in the Western World.

We are all of us familiar with the descendants of the Africans transported across the Atlantic Ocean to work on the plantations of the New World. We refer to such people today as Caribbeans or African-Americans and their history has in the last few years brought about demands for recognition of the ill effects of colonization and the slave trade. Statues have been removed, street names changed and university curricula 'decolonized' in the interests of making atonement for the past. The Black Lives Matter protests of 2020 helped stimulate this process. What though of the descendants of the black African slaves whose ancestors were carried in the opposite direction, east across the Indian Ocean? The fate of such individuals was every bit as undesirable as that of the slaves taken to America and the Caribbean, but they have been lost to history.

Once Arab influence was firmly established on the East African coast, they took over the trade routes which had been established by Axum. The demand for ivory and slaves was as strong as ever and it hardly made any difference to those in India and Sri Lanka whether they purchased these useful commodities from one part of Africa or another. So it was that during the eighth and ninth centuries AD Arab ships were plying the seas with their cargoes of slaves. Some of these unfortunates were destined to work on plantations, but in India some were recruited into the army.

Geneticists have over the last few years provided us with a great deal of new evidence which enables us to piece together human history in a scientific way, free of the effects of national prejudice and no longer reliant upon fragmentary and debatable archaeological evidence. The study of several ethnic groups in India has provided us with a perfect example of this. In three provinces of western India live a distinct ethnic group called the Siddis. In Gujarat, Karnataka and Andhra Pradesh one sees people whose skins are noticeably darker than everybody else and whose features sometimes tend more towards the African than South Asia. There is another large population, numbering perhaps a quarter of a million, living in Pakistan. These are the descendants of the slaves brought to India by Arab slave traders and, in later centuries, the Portuguese. The earliest historical mention of black slaves being brought to India indicates that they first arrived in 628 AD, with many more reaching the country during the Muslim conquest in the early eighth century (Pandya, 2002). There are brief mentions of the arrival of other black slaves in the eleventh century and more extensive records from the thirteenth century AD (Shah *et al*, 2011). Some of these slaves came to India overland and had previously been trafficked north into the Middle East, probably via Egypt. Others though had been taken by ship from the Swahili Coast.

There can indeed be few people in the West who are unaware that those we now call Caribbeans or African-Americans are the descendants of slaves who were taken from their homes and shipped to another continent to work for nothing other than their food, as though they were beasts of burden such as oxen or donkeys. We are not allowed to forget this cruel injustice done to their ancestors and making reparations, or at the very least displaying contrition, for the sins of white European ancestors is now *de rigeur* for anybody in Britain or the United States who wishes to be seen as progressive or humane.

The situation relating to the distant relatives of those who were carried away from Africa in the opposite direction is very different.

It is exceedingly unlikely that anybody in Europe and America, other than professional anthropologists or other academics, have even heard of the Siddis. They were living in the Indian subcontinent a thousand years before any black slaves landed in the New World and their numbers were swelled over the centuries by new arrivals taken to India by the Arabs and later the Portuguese. The Siddis are sometimes known as Habshis. This indicated one of the routes whereby their ancestors came to India. 'Habshi' is the word used for a captain of the ships which traded between Ethiopia and India at the time when the Axumite empire was in the ascendant. Others refer to them as Afro-Indians. Whatever name is used, these are people who form a distinct ethnic group and have done so for over a thousand years. Although they wear the same clothes as everybody around them – the women wear saris or Shalwar kameez – and follow similar religions, the Siddis also have their own customs which they have followed since leaving Africa all those years ago. These too give a clue as to which part of Africa they originated from. Gujarati Siddis, for instance, have a form of music called Goma. This derives from the Swahili word *ngoma*, meaning drums (Jayasuriya and Pankhurst, 2003). Goma is based upon African drumming rhythms. One other interesting point is that just as with African–Americans and Caribbeans, athletics and sport are seen by the Siddis as a traditional route out of poverty and deprivation.

Sometimes, cultural and linguistic evidence can be mistaken or distorted, but this cannot be the case with analysis of the genetic heritage of individuals. In 2011 *The American Journal of Human Genetics* published the results of a massive study of the genomes of Siddis in India (Shah *et al*, 2011). They found that the greatest contribution to the heritage of the Siddis was some centuries later than the Arab and Axumite slave trading. In the sixteenth century, the Portuguese claimed large chunks of East Africa for their own and began taking over the slave trade from Zanzibar and the Swahili Coast from the Arabs. It was from this period, the sixteenth to nineteenth centuries, that the researchers, who included David Reich from Harvard, discovered the most traces. They were able to establish that the flow of genes with the Siddis had tended to be towards their group from the wider Indian population, rather than the other way round. Although there is a mild taboo in Siddi culture against marrying out of the group, some do take Indian or Pakistani wives.

The Siddis show how extensive was the slave trade between Africa and India and also the great length of time for which it was carried out. By way of comparison, the better-known transatlantic slave trade did not really get going until the seventeenth century and had ended by the nineteenth. That carried out between East Africa and the Indian subcontinent, by way of contrast, lasted from the third century AD and continued for at least another 1,500 years. In other words, it lasted six or seven times as long as the slave trade which took place between Africa and the New World.

In addition to the Siddis of India and Pakistan, there is another group in that part of the world who have a separate, African identity which dates back to the days of the slave trade. These are the Kaffirs of Sri Lanka. Before going any further, it might be as well to explain and justify the use of the word 'kaffir', which is today widely regarded as a racial slur. Some readers might recall that in 2021 there was a fuss about the name of a garden plant, known for many years as Kaffir Lilies. After the Black Lives Matter protests the previous year, there had been a heightened sensitivity to anything which might be interpreted as a racial slur and Kaffir Lilies fitted the bill perfectly. In South Africa, white people referred to blacks as 'kaffirs' during the years of apartheid.

The word 'kaffir' is a corruption of the Arabic *kuffar*, which is a derogatory term for an unbeliever; somebody who is not a Muslim. The expression became common on the Swahili Coast and so found its way down into South Africa. This is why Kaffir Lilies are problematic to some militant activists. The case is quite different in Sri Lanka, where Kaffir is the term chosen by the people to describe themselves. The Kaffirs of Sri Lanka, who once spoke a distinctive creole based on Portuguese with elements of African languages in the same way that Swahili was formed, are the descendants of Portuguese traders and African slaves who settled in what was then the kingdom of Ceylon. They came to the country from the sixteenth century and after a century or two formed a distinct group with their own language and customs. Intermarriage has reduced the Kaffirs in number since then and they are reduced to three small communities, consisting of no more than a thousand people in total.

Although this was not a colonization, an increasing number of Arabs came to live in this part of Africa and when the Portuguese arrived in 1498, at the same time that Columbus was making his first expedition across the Atlantic, they found a strong Arab element to the societies along the coast. Indeed, it was soon discovered that the Arabs had been very industrious in their trade in slaves, for when they reached Sri Lanka and decided to add that too to the Portuguese empire, it was clear that the Arabs had rather beaten them to it.

These were the great days of Portuguese colonialism and it will hardly surprise anybody to learn that they claimed Zanzibar and the coast facing it as Portuguese territory. We are all familiar with the British Empire, French Empire, Spanish Empire and so on, that we sometimes forget that the Portuguese had one of the most extensive empires in the world. From Brazil to East Africa and all the way to China, the Portuguese managed to hang on to their overseas possessions for longer than many European countries. The Indian state of Goa, for example, was held by Portugal for 450 years, from the early sixteenth century until 1961. At this point, the Indian army invaded Goa and incorporated it into their own country. The territory of Macau, near Hong Kong, was not handed over to Chinese control until 1999. It was in East Africa though that the Portuguese clung on most fiercely to their colonial possessions, only surrendering them to African control following a military coup in Portugal in 1974. These were the areas from which Portugal had been enslaving people and then taking them east or west as the need arose. We shall deal with the Portuguese slave trade across the Atlantic to Brazil in a later chapter, but for now we must see what they were up to in East Africa in the years leading up to the seventeenth century.

A major motivation for Portuguese colonialism was the spice trade from Asia. This was in the medieval period dominated by the Arabs, because cargoes travelling overland from India and China had to pass through the Middle East to reach Europe. Finding maritime routes to the Far East was a way to break this stranglehold on trade. It will be remembered that Columbus' first voyage across the Atlantic was sponsored by Portugal for this very reason, as a possible way of reaching Asia swiftly. Alas, it was not to be and so the longer passage around the southern tip of Africa and then across the Indian Ocean was the way that the Portuguese finally settled on for getting to India and China. It was for this reason that staging posts on the African coast were required, safe havens where ships could put into harbour and stock up on water and food without the risk of a hostile reception from the natives.

The earliest exploratory voyages of the Portuguese merchants who were seeking for spices, gold and anything else which they could then carry back to their own country and sell at a profit, were made by ships which were unladen. There was space on board to stow all the things which they hoped to pick up, but did not think it worth taking any goods with them. This of course changed when they reached East Africa and found a thriving slave trade already being run by Arabs in which ships left each end of the route fully laden.

So it was that the Portuguese began taking slaves from Africa to the east and west. We shall be looking closely at the Atlantic slave trade between West Africa and the Americas later on, but for now it is enough to observe that the Portuguese took a huge number of African slaves to their colony of Brazil and that by the time they had finished, Africans made up no less than a third of the population of the country (Haywood, 2008). By comparison, the number of slaves taken from East Africa by the Portuguese was modest enough, but still sufficient that there are today hundreds of thousands of Afro-Indians or Siddis in India, descendants of the slaves taken there by the Arabs and Portuguese.

That the slave trade from East Africa to India and the Far East was not a huge commercial success for Portugal was in a sense irrelevant, for the Portuguese Crown was playing a longer and more far-sighted plan than merely the short-term profit from consignments of slaves being sold to this or that Indian potentate. Taking over the Arab trade routes, which included of course the shipments of slaves from Africa, was part of a geopolitical strategy designed to break the Muslim monopoly on trade with the Far East. The sixteenth and seventeenth centuries were the time when the struggle between Islam and Christianity was reaching a climax, with sea battles in the Mediterranean and Ottoman incursions first into Eastern Europe and then further and further west, culminating in the Siege of Vienna in 1683.

Debates today about European colonialism in Africa and the transatlantic slave trade all too often neglect to take into account the struggle between Christendom and the Muslim world. This means that much of what was happening in Africa during what is sometimes described as the Age of Exploration is almost impossible to understand. Without fully taking into account the fervent desire by Christians and Muslims for control of routes by land and sea and also the desire to occupy each other's territory, a complex subject such as slavery in Africa will be impossible to understand.

Our study of Africa has now brought us to the sixteenth century, the time when African slaves began to be taken across the Atlantic Ocean to North and South America. Before looking in detail at the effect that this traffic had on slavery as it was already being practised in Africa, we turn once more to the north of the continent and see what sources the so-called Barbary States, which were by this time provinces of the Ottoman Empire, tapped for slaves.

Chapter 6

The North African Slave Trade in the Sixteenth and Seventeenth Centuries

It is a very strange thing, but for all the modern agonising over the slave trade, nobody seems eager to think about the fact that Europe was raided for slaves to a far greater extent in the medieval period than was Africa. At that time, most of the slaves in the Arab world were Slavs from Russia and Eastern Europe, but by the middle of the sixteenth century, another source of slaves was being exploited, which was Western European countries such as Italy, Spain and England. The slavers involved in this trade, who were known variously as corsairs or Barbary Pirates, sailed from ports like Tunis or Algiers and then descended upon seaside villages in Italy, France and Spain. The inhabitants were rounded up, loaded onto the ships and then carried off to the slave markets in the ports from which the ships had come.

The word 'corsair' has a romantic air about it, even though most of us do not really have any clear idea what the expression actually means and tend usually to see it as being synonymous with 'pirate'. The two things are theoretically quite separate, although in practice they were often indistinguishable from each other. In the sixteenth century, and for hundreds of years later, some states commissioned private citizens commanding ships to carry out acts of war. This is really an instance of that most modern of phenomena, privatisation. Countries like England and France were able to maintain a relatively modest navy and then engage individuals who would supplement these naval forces as and when they might be required. Those in command of such ships were known as privateers. Famous English sea captains and explorers like Francis Drake and John Hawkins operated as privateers at times during the Elizabethan Era. Privateers were provided with what is known as a letter of marque. This specified the nationality of ships which could be attacked and also limited the commission to a certain length of time. Of course, many enemy ships were carrying gold or other valuable cargo and the privateer was free to loot any enemy vessels which he captured. The ruler of the country which had provided the letter of marque was entitled to a percentage of the plunder.

Of course, one nation's privateers might very well be regarded by opposing nations as little better than pirates. This is certainly how Francis Drake was viewed by the Spanish. It is also true that some privateers also attacked ships belonging to countries not named in the letter of marque which they carried, putting them in effect in the category of pirates.

Part of the reason why we do not remember the centuries during which Europe was at the mercy of these African slave traders is that when we hear the word 'pirate' it conjures up a vision of Long John Silver or Captain Hook, rather than Muslim merchants carrying off white families into slavery. The expression Barbary Pirate, named after the old name for North Africa, the Barbary Coast, has served to conceal the true nature of what was happening in Europe. A slight detour into the world of etymology, the study of the derivation and origins of words, is perhaps called for at this point. The original inhabitants of North Africa were the Berbers. Barbary is a corruption of Berber.

The raids by the Barbary Pirates took place at the same time that the Ottoman Empire was expanding westwards into Europe and at times it was difficult to distinguish between mercantile expeditions undertaken for monetary gain and probing attacks at sea which were of a piece with the long-term strategy of the Turks, aimed at conquering Europe and turning it into another part of the Caliphate. Indeed, the actions of the corsairs are sometimes referred to as the Marine Jihad (Syed, 2011). The attack on Malta in 1551 provides us with a perfect illustration of this point and it is difficult at times to say whether we are seeing an act of war or a commercial enterprise.

The Ottomans were inching towards the heart of Europe on land, nibbling away remorselessly at that part of the continent which we now know as Bosnia, Serbia, Croatia and Hungary. This process would bring the Turkish army eventually to the gates of Vienna. At the same time, parts of southern Europe were under pressure from the so-called 'pirates' of the Barbary Coast. In 1526, the Ottoman army attacked the Kingdom of Hungary, defeating it at the Battle of Mohacs. This brought them within striking distance of Austria, then a major power in Europe. A large part of Eastern Europe was now occupied by Muslims (Hibbert, 1970). This was a slow and steady erosion of Christian Europe and those waging this religious crusade felt that history, and God, were on their side. There was no particular hurry. Having moved the boundaries of the Caliphate forward on land by a few hundred miles, the sultan in Constantinople turned his attention to the island of Malta, which although at that time a stronghold of Christianity had in the past been occupied by Muslim Arabs. This of course explains why Maltese is the only European language to be based upon Arabic.

The main island of Malta was held by a Catholic military order, known commonly as the Knights Hospitaller or, more correctly, the Order of the Knights of the Hospital of Saint John of Jerusalem. If the Turks of the Ottoman Empire wished to move further into Europe, then mastery of the sea was important. Capturing Malta would give the Ottomans a useful naval base from which they would be able to launch attacks on Italy and Spain. Before this could be done, the Knights Hospitaller would have to be dislodged. In 1551, a fleet under the command of Sinan Pasha anchored of the Maltese coast and landed 10,000 troops. These men marched on the town of Birgu, which had been fortified by the Knights Hospitaller and looked capable of withstanding a prolonged siege. Having no appetite for this and being in any case ill-prepared for such a venture, the Turks moved on to the island's capital, Mdina. This town had been reinforced and since the Ottoman army had really only enough provisions for a brief period of warfare, they retreated back to their ships.

While all this was going on a Barbary corsair by the name of Turgut Reis had turned up and realized that a fantastic business opportunity now presented itself. In addition to the main island of Malta, there was a smaller one called Gozo. With the Catholic troops all massed in the fortified towns, the population of Gozo was left quite undefended. With the help of some of Sinan Pasha's ships, Turgut Reis attacked Gozo and seized the entire population, other than one monk and a few dozen old people who were too aged and incapable to be any use as slaves. In all, 6,000 men, women and children were taken prisoner and taken off to the slave markets of Tripoli. The sacking of Gozo is a perfect illustration of the way in which it is impossible to draw a clear distinction between slave raids and orthodox military expeditions in the Mediterranean at this time. Describing the Barbary Pirates as part of the Marine Jihad really is apposite.

One of the strange things about the slavery in North Africa is that although the trade consisted almost solely of white Europeans, most people today have never even heard of it. This is odd, because some fairly well-known people were involved in it in one capacity or another. Take Miguel Cervantes, the author of *Don Quixote*, which is often called the first European novel. A coalition of Catholic nations, known as the Holy League, wanted to prevent further Ottoman expansion into Europe and they put together a formidable fleet which consisted mainly of Spanish and Venetian ships. On 7 October 1571 they clashed with a Turkish fleet off the coast of Greece, an engagement known as the Battle of Lepanto. Cervantes, who had joined the Spanish marines the previous year, fought in this battle.

For five years, Miguel Cervantes fought against the Ottoman navy as a soldier of the Holy League. It was when he was sailing home at the end of his military service that disaster struck. On 26 September 1575, the ship he was in was attacked by corsairs and he and the rest of the crew were taken to Algiers and sold as slaves (Thorlby, 1969). Cervantes spent the next five years as a slave, until he was ransomed by the religious order of the Trinitarians. Ransom was another way that the slave trade was profitable to the corsairs of North Africa. If they happened to capture somebody with a wealthy family, then it was sometimes possible to sell a captive back for a larger sum than the person would fetch in the slave market.

We pause at this point and consider how strange it is that when a film was made called *12 Years a Slave*, it was a tremendous hit at the box office, winning three Oscars. It tells the story of a black man who is kidnapped in New York and then sold into slavery in one of the southern states of America. Such a narrative fits in perfectly with our current historical and cultural framework and the idea of capturing a black man and selling him into slavery is just the kind of wicked thing we can imagine happening in the past. Consider for a moment though, if you will, the idea of a biographical film about the life of the author of *Don Quixote* called *Five Years a Slave*. The idea of a white European being kidnapped and sold into slavery in Africa does not tie in at all with what we think we know about slavery and such a film about the trials of Cervantes would seem like a bizarre fantasy.

As the years passed, the slave traders began to travel further afield in their quest for new slaves. Mastery of the Mediterranean was not really achieved, because of the organized opposition of the Christian countries of Europe. This was strong enough to prevent Ottoman fleets from operating at will, if not to wholly deter individual ships making hit-and-run attacks in search of slaves. As the seventeenth century drew on, the main thrust of Ottoman expansion was on land rather than at sea, culminating in the Siege of Vienna in 1683. This was the high-water mark of Muslim expansion into Europe.

The provinces of the Barbary Coast were often, in effect, independent nations, although they owed allegiance to the sultan in Constantinople. The activities of the corsairs, or state-sponsored pirates, who operated from the ports of North Africa at times coincided with the Ottoman strategy for the conquest of Christian Europe, although for much of the time these rovers of the sea were motivated solely by self-interest. As the Mediterranean became less and less the main theatre in the struggle between Islam and Christianity and the armies of the sultan edged slowly forward through the Balkans, consolidating their territorial gains as they went, it happened in the seventeenth century that the navies of Christian nations gained the upper hand in the Mediterranean. This inevitably made life more hazardous for the corsairs and they began searching further afield for slaves, in those stretches of sea where they ran less chance of coming up against heavily armed Spanish or Venetian ships. They began to slip past Gibraltar into the Atlantic and from there up into the English Channel and North Sea.

Ships belonging to Christian countries were being targeted by the corsairs as well at this time. There was an increase in trade between Europe and various countries in Asia and much of the goods were transported overland to ports in the Levant and then taken from there by ship across the Mediterranean to Europe (Greengrass, 2014). This meant that such merchant vessels were tempting for both their cargoes and also crews who could be sold into slavery. The fate of those captured in this way was exceedingly grim. Perhaps the worst outcome was that they would end up as galley slaves.

Galleys are large ships which are rowed by oars. In the sixteenth century they were widely used as both warships and merchant vessels by the Christian nations of Europe and the Muslim states of North Africa and Turkey. The oars for galleys were about 35ft long and had the mass of a modern telegraph pole. It was accordingly far beyond the capabilities of one man to pull such an oar and so between three and seven men were assigned to each one. All had to pull in perfect unison if the ships were to make a good speed.

The point about galleys is that they will only work efficiently if every single man is seated at an oar and working constantly to his maximum effort. If half the rowers were out of their places because they were eating, drinking, urinating or opening their bowels, then the ship will not be able to operate effectively. For this reason, it was found to be better to crew this type of vessel with slaves, rather than free men. This introduced a new problem though, in that such slaves, having nothing to lose, might be inclined to launch a mutiny and try and take over the ship if not constantly watched and carefully guarded. With perhaps 50 oars to each ship and around five men to each oar meant that there were 250 desperate men who would surely be thinking continuously of a revolt to gain their freedom. The means adopted to nullify this threat were horrific in the extreme.

Galley slaves were shackled permanently to the benches at which they toiled. They were not unchained at any time, for any reason at all, unless they should happen to die of exhaustion. This meant that if they wished to defecate or urinate then they had no option but to do so where they were sitting. Little wonder that it was said in the sixteenth century that a galley crewed by slaves could quite literally be smelled a mile away (Bridge, 1988). This is no exaggeration. Imagine, if you will, hundreds of men compelled to open their bowels and void their bladders where they were sitting, day after day for years at a time. There was of course no water available for washing and so added to the appalling stench of the human waste, in which they would be ankle deep, would be the smell of unwashed bodies, all generating copious quantities of sweat as they laboured at some of the most strenuous work imaginable.

The galley slaves were not unchained at night so that they could lay down to sleep. Freeing them for a period of sleep would have given the slaves an opportunity to rebel or perhaps even to jump overboard in an attempt to escape or kill themselves. This was not a risk worth taking and so they were left shackled to their places for 24 hours a day, having to sleep upright as best they might.

The number of slaves needed for the galleys of both the Ottoman Empire and the Christian nations of Europe was enormous. We can get some idea of the numbers involved by looking at the last major battle between galleys powered by slaves, which took place off the coast of Greece in 1571. A group of Catholic countries in Europe, alarmed at the expansion of the Ottoman in their direction, formed a coalition called the Holy League. Both the Ottoman Empire and the Holy League, which included among its members Spain and the city-state of Venice, had large fleets of galleys. On 7 October 1571 the two fleets clashed at the Gulf of Patras. The ensuing naval engagement became known as the Battle of Lepanto, because that was the name of the port from which the Ottoman forces had sailed. It was a victory for the Holy League and after defeating the Ottoman ships, the galley slaves who had been rowing them were freed. There were an astonishing 13,000 of them. This gives some idea of the huge demand for such slaves; a demand which the Barbary corsairs were satisfying. Illustrations 18 and 19 show Barbary pirates.

Just as with the corsairs of Europe, the ships sailing from ports in North Africa were to a certain extent operating on behalf of the state. It was accepted that in return for being able to use the ports of Algiers, Tripoli or Tunis, the rulers of those provinces or countries would be entitled to a proportion of the treasure and slaves taken during the course of their activities. As a general rule, an eighth of the slaves captured had to be handed over to the state. One man who was later released from captivity in Algiers described the slave market to which European prisoners were taken on arrival. He grossly overestimated the rank of the Ottoman governor of Algiers by terming him the 'king', but otherwise his account is accurate and accords well enough with other evidence.

> This market was where the local king had his seat, so that he would have the shortest way there, because, as I was told by those who had been there a long time, their king took from the captured people every eighth man, every eighth woman, and every eighth child . . . (Hreinsson and Nichols, 2016)

It is hard to say whether those taken into service by the state fared better or worse than the ones who ended up being sold to private purchasers. The state slaves were sometimes sent to the galleys, a dreadful fate. Others though ended up as the equivalent of clerical workers. There was also a wide variation in the conditions of service for men and women bought by ordinary merchants and so on.

Some villages on the coasts of Italy, Spain and France were abandoned at this time, as people moved inland to avoid the risk of being taken by slavers. However, the raids were not confined to the Mediterranean, but extended into the North Atlantic and English Channel. Fortunately for the corsairs sailing from the Barbary Coast, England was not in the early years of the seventeenth century a formidable sea power. King James VI of Scotland, who had in 1603 acceded to the throne of England as James I of that country, had no particular interest in the navy. The fleet which had less than 15 years earlier defeated the formidable Spanish Armada, became neglected and, to use the modern jargon, no longer 'fit for purpose'. The ill effects of this could hardly escape the notice of a seagoing people like the English.

Although the corsairs from the Barbary Coast were quite willing and able to land and take prisoners from villages and towns, many of the slaves whom they seized were sailors from fishing boats and merchant ships. England had always depended upon the sea to supplement its agricultural produce and many coastal towns had fleets which sailed the English Channel, North Sea and even the Atlantic. These boats were easy prey for the slavers who began to infest the coastal waters which surrounded the British Isles. The extent of the problem may be seen when we learn that between 1609 and 1616, no fewer than 466 English ships were boarded and their crews taken off to be sold in the slave markets of Tunis and Algiers (Brown, 1970). By 1625, the year in which James I died and was succeeded as king of England by his son Charles, matters had reached a very low ebb indeed.

In April 1625, four ships sailing from English ports were taken by corsairs; three from Cornwall and one from Devon. From then on, the situation deteriorated sharply, until by August that year, the slavers were not limiting their attacks to shipping, but were actually landing in England to make slaves of those living in coastal villages. A raiding party landed, for instance at Mount's Bay in Cornwall. When the local inhabitants saw the ships anchored in the bay, they fled to the local church in the hope that it would provide sanctuary. The African slave traders had no respect for any Christian place of worship though and broke into the church, dragging out more than sixty people and loading them onto the waiting ships. All those taken in this raid ended up in the slave markets of North Africa.

On 12 August, the Mayor of Plymouth appealed for help to the Privy Council in London. He wrote that in just 10 days, twenty-seven ships had been boarded and the crews taken off into slavery; over 200 men in total (Dalrymple, 2004). His cry for help read as follows;

> The Mayor of Plymouth writes that there are general fears for the ships from Virginia and Newfoundland. Twenty-seven ships and 200 persons had been taken by Turkish pirates in ten days. (*Calendar of State Papers*, 1860)

The mention of 'Turkish pirates' requires some explanation, for the men conducting these operations were not Turkish at all. Because the various nations of North Africa were technically provinces of the Ottoman Empire, any ships associated with the Ottomans in any way were customarily referred as being Turkish. 'Turk' was in fact used as a synonym at that time for 'Muslim' and those converting to Islam were said to have 'turned Turk'.

The Mayor of Plymouth was not the only person in the West Country of England who was writing to London at that time to alert them to what was going on. That same month, August 1625, the Mayor of Poole is recorded as followed in the correspondence of the time,

> Mayor of Poole to the Privy Council. Unless measures are taken, the Newfoundland fleet of 250 sail, having on board four or five thousand men of the western parts, will be surprised by the Turkish pirates. (*Calendar of State Papers*, 1860)

That both mayors mention Newfoundland is significant. It was not merely a question of a few fisherfolk who were being inconvenienced and even kidnapped. There were so many slavers now in and around English territorial waters that communication with the American colonies was in danger of being disrupted.

Charles I was no more interested in strengthening the navy than his father had been. So ineffectual was this navy by the late 1620s, that a truly incredible state of affairs arose. We are most of us aware that the European slave traders who went to West Africa to acquire slaves to take to the Caribbean and American colonies had bases in Africa from which they operated. Some of these were little more than stockades where they kept the slaves whom they had purchased penned up like animals, until a ship arrived which would carry them across the Atlantic Ocean. It may seem beyond belief, but the African slavers who were harrying the British Isles at this time also established such a base in a strategic waterway within sight of the English mainland.

For most of us, the phrase 'pirate island' conjures up images of a tropical sea and golden beach, fringed with palm trees. The island of Lundy, which is in the Bristol Channel and lies about 12 miles off the coast of Devon, was a pirate island of a very different kind. In 1627 a fleet of corsairs from Morocco took control of Lundy and remained there, on and off, for years (Milton, 2005). This was a convenient base from which to launch expeditions against other parts of the British Isles, besides Cornwall and Devon. Not only the British Isles either. In the summer of 1627 ships sailed from Lundy to Iceland, arriving on 20 June. A couple of dozen people from a village on the coast were taken prisoner and transported back to Lundy and then on to Algiers. Two weeks later, a larger group of ships from Algiers also arrived off the coast of Iceland and took away 350 men, women and children. By all accounts, they behaved with great cruelty,

> Then they began to set fire to the houses. There was a woman there who could not walk, whom they had captured easily.

Her, they threw on the fire, along with her two-year-old baby. When she and the poor child screamed and called to God for help, the wicked Turks bellowed with laughter. They stuck both child and mother with the sharp points of their spears, forcing them into the fire, and even stabbed fiercely at the poor, burning bodies. (Hreinsson and Nichols, 2016)

In short, though the Mediterranean had become a little less comfortable than it had once been for activities of this kind, the wide expanses of the oceans beyond Gibraltar more than compensated for this.

Perhaps the most famous incident of those times was what became known as the sacking of Baltimore. In 1631 Baltimore was a small village on the southernmost tip of Ireland. In June of that year, some corsairs sailing out of Algiers came across a lone fishing boat near Ireland. On board was a man called John Hackett, whom they took prisoner. Anxious to avoid being carried off to Africa and sold as a slave, Hackett told the men who took him that if they would agree to free him, he would guide their ships to a quiet and sleepy village which they would be able to catch completely unawares and so capture as many people as they wished.

John Hackett went ashore with the raiding-party, so as to guide them to Baltimore. He was then allowed to go his own way. A dramatic poem by the Victorian author Thomas Osborn Davis paints a vivid picture of the events which followed,

All, all asleep within each roof along that rocky street,
And these must be the lover's friends, with gently gliding feet-
A stifled gasp, a dreamy noise! 'The roof is in a flame!'
From out their beds and to their doors rush maid and sire and dame,
And meet upon the threshold stone the gleaming sabre's fall,
And o'er each black and bearded face the white or crimson shawl,
The yell of 'Allah!' breaks above the prayer, and shriek, and roar:
O blessed God! The Algerine is lord of Baltimore!

The Algerine was indeed lord of Baltimore that night and a total of eighty-nine women and children, together with twenty men, were taken prisoner and endured a journey of 38 days before finally reaching Algiers. The children were forcibly separated from their mothers and, for the most part, they converted to Islam (O Domhnaill, 2015).

Many readers, particularly those in Britain, will probably be surprised to learn that slavers operating from African ports were raiding the British Isles more or less at will and carrying people off to the slave markets of Algiers, Tripoli and Tunis. This complete lack of awareness of the slaving raids made on England and Ireland during the sixteenth and seventeenth centuries has been described by Professor Esra of the University of Exeter as 'cultural erasure' (*Daily Telegraph*, 2017). It provides a neat illustration of the point made in the Introduction to this book, that when *the* slave trade is mentioned, our thoughts turn unbidden to black Africans being transported across the Atlantic by white men. The idea that white men from Europe were themselves being snatched from their homes and carried off to an African slave market seems to go against all that we think we know about the slave trade.

There is something a little odd about the lack of knowledge about the white slaves of North Africa. After all, it is not as though the historical record of this phenomenon has been hidden or censored. References to such slaves are to be found often enough in the writings of the time. The matter is even referred to in the diaries of Samuel Pepys. After a visit to a pub one lunchtime, Pepys wrote at some length about what he had been told. The casual and matter-of-fact way in which he wrote suggests that there was nothing at all remarkable in what he had heard that that Friday lunchtime on 8 February 1661.

> At the office all the morning. At noon to the Exchange to meet Mr Warren the timber merchant, but could not meet with him. Here I met with many sea commanders, and among other Captain Cuttle, and Curtis, and Mootham,

and I, went to the Fleece Tavern to drink; and there we spent till four o'clock, telling stories of Algiers, and the manner of life of slaves there! And truly Captn. Mootham and Mr Dawes (who have been both slaves there) did make me fully acquainted with their condition there: as, how they eat nothing buy bread and water. At their redemption they pay so much for the water they drink at the public fontaynes, during their being slaves. How they are beat upon the soles of their feet and their bellies at the liberty of their padron. How they are all, at night, called into their master's Bagnard; and there they lie. How the poorest men use their slaves the best. How some rogues do live well, if they do invent to bring their masters in so much a week by their industry or theft; and then they are put to no other work at all. And theft there is counted no great crime at all. (Pepys, 1661)

That Pepys writes of Englishmen who were enslaved in Algiers so casually indicates that he knew all about this form of slavery and was not at all surprised by the tales the two men related. As to why this type of slavery has been generally forgotten today, that is another question and may have something to do with the fact that the narrative of black slaves in the Americas and the Caribbean has by degrees come to be the only kind of slavery which anybody cares to know about.

The capture and trade in slaves captured from either European ships or by raids on the mainland continued for another 150 years after Samuel Pepys wrote in his diary of meeting those former slaves. The way in which it came to an end is rather circuitous, with many loose ends and surprising twists and turns. After the English Civil War ended with the triumph of Oliver Cromwell and the Parliamentary forces, Cromwell determined that whatever King Charles and his father may have been willing to put up with, he would tolerate no nonsense from a bunch of pirates, and pirates who were not even Christians at that. Cromwell was of course very hot in his faith and although he without doubt found it irksome to see English ships seized on the high seas and his authority as a ruler set at naught, the fact that those carrying out these outrageous acts were avowed enemies of the Christian religion was also an important factor in his attitude towards the Barbary States.

As Lord Protector of the Commonwealth, as Cromwell was styled, he was the nearest thing that Britain now had to a monarch. Some European countries though regarded Oliver Cromwell as an upstart and regicide. He decided that he would demonstrate the strength of the country which he now ruled by mounting an expedition to discourage anybody from interfering with ships flying the nation's flag. The aim was both to strike a blow at the heathens who were still raiding isolated villages in remote parts of England and Ireland and also to show Europe that despite having no king, Britain was still a force to be reckoned with. The perfect opportunity presented itself when an English ship in the Mediterranean was captured by ships sailing out of Tunis and the crew taken to a slave market and sold there.

At the end of 1654 General-at-Sea (the term used at that time in the navy rather than admiral) Robert Blake was despatched to the Mediterranean with sixteen ships. He was authorized if necessary to launch a war against the Ottoman provinces of North Africa. Other countries which had been suffering from the predations of the Barbary corsairs watched with interest.

Blake arrived at Tunis on 8 February 1655 and anchored near the town. He then sent word that the English sailors who had lately been taken prisoner were to be released. To this peremptory demand, he received a flat refusal. Although nobody could have guessed it, the rules of naval warfare were about to be rewritten. The corsairs' ships lay in a harbour called Porto Farina, which lay a few miles to the north of Tunis. After some further negotiations, Robert Blake ordered an attack. That it was not merely a bunch of pirates with whom he had to deal was clear. There were fortified shore batteries with heavy artillery at Porto Farina and a castle nearby.

The result of the battle was a resounding victory for the British forces. Not only were the Tunisian ships set on fire, but the shore batteries were also taken out by firing from ships. This was the first time such a feat had ever been achieved, all previous actions of this kind having entailed landing forces to deal with fortified emplacements. Naval warfare would never be the same again. After dealing with Tunis, Blake sailed on to Algiers, but the man in charge there had no appetite for fighting and readily agreed to free all the slaves from England.

The British expedition of 1655 showed the rest of Europe how it was possible to deal with the menace from North Africa. France launched a similar attack on Algiers in 1682, shelling the city and causing an immense amount of damage. This was all very well, but military adventures of this kind were very expensive and uncertain. It would bankrupt a country to keep sending fleets sailing off to the Mediterranean every few months to inflict another lesson on the Barbary States and none of these sharp lessons seemed to act as a permanent deterrent to the slavers. It was ultimately found to be cheaper and more convenient just to pay the men in charge of Tunis and Algiers a certain sum of money each year so that they would bring ships sailing from their ports into line and stop attacks on the shipping of those countries which offered annually what became known as 'tribute'. It may seem odd that militarily strong nations should behave in this way and hand over large sums of cash each year simply to ensure that their commercial ships were not molested, but it actually made good sense.

The British had already show their teeth and nobody doubted that they were capable of returning to Tunis and Algiers and bombarding both cities if they felt aggrieved. However, it was cheaper and easier simply to send a sum of money each year to those in charge of the cities, who would then make sure that none of their ships were troubled. This annual 'tribute' was viewed by the British as being akin to a tax or toll. There was another advantage to the arrangement which was that British mercantile shipping was able to trade freely in the Mediterranean, but that of countries which had not reached similar accommodations with the Barbary States was not. This served to reduce competition in trade.

The slave trade in North Africa continued in this way for a century or so, with the number of Europeans taken as slaves greatly reduced. The end of the white slaves there more or less coincided with the British abolition of the slave trade in her empire and it was to be the newly independent United States which dealt it the final blow. We shall be finding out about this in Chapter 8.

Of course, the seventeenth century was the time when the transatlantic slave trade really took off in a big way and this will be the subject of the next chapter.

Chapter 7

The Triangular Trade in Full Swing

Most of us are familiar with the concept of transportation to Australia, a punishment inflicted on convicted criminals in Britain during the first half of the nineteenth century, often as a supposedly milder alternative to hanging. The conditions under which such people laboured were harsh and they were subject to flogging if they attempted to escape from the penal colonies to which they had been sent. Although Australia is well known as a destination in this context, it was across the Atlantic that the first penal transportations from Britain took place. Some were sent to the American colonies and others to the Caribbean. In 1634, for instance, 86 per cent of the inhabitants of Barbados were white Europeans. Many of these had been transported to the island as a punishment, but others were indentured servants. This latter expression needs some explanation.

Such was the desperate poverty in Britain and Ireland during the seventeenth and eighteenth centuries that some people would take any steps to secure food, lodgings and a new start in life. One way of doing this was to sign a contract with an employer in the colonies, binding oneself to work for this person for a set number of years, typically seven. In return, the employer or master would pay for passage across the Atlantic and guarantee living quarters and food while the person so 'indentured' worked for him. There were several drawbacks to this scheme. For one thing, indentured servants lost all their rights and became little better than slaves, being unable to leave their employment and also subject in some cases to physical punishment by whipping. They had no recourse to law.

Something which was seldom fully explained to those who signed up in this way for a new start in the Americas or Caribbean was that their master could sell the contract on to another person. Some such servants found themselves arriving in Barbados and being auctioned at a market to the highest bidder. Conditions for many indentured white labourers on the plantations were worse than those of black slaves. The reason was simply a matter of economics. Black slaves were like expensive farm animals, a working sheepdog or horse for example. The owner could expect to get a lifetime of work from them and the longer they lived, then the more work would be done. There was an incentive in preserving their health and ensuring that they had sufficient to eat. This was not at all the case with indentured servants. Their master knew that he had only a set number of years to wring as much labour from these unfortunate individuals as he could. There was every reason therefore to work them as hard as could be done and to skimp on food and also medical attention if they fell ill. Many of these people did not live long enough to obtain their freedom at the end of their seven years of bondage. In the seventeenth century, a French writer observed the abuses of this system and said:

> There were masters so cruel that they were forbidden to purchase any more; and I knew one at Guadeloupe who had buried more than fifty upon his plantation, whom he had killed by hard work, and neglect when they were sick. The cruelty proceeded from their having them for some years only, which made them spare the Negro rather than these poor creatures! (Everett, 1997)

In the course of time, it became known in Britain that there was more to indentured servitude than appeared on the surface and fewer people were willing to sign up to such arrangements. This led to healthy young men in ports being seized by stealth and carried on board ships heading across the Atlantic, a system similar to the press gangs of the navy. By the end of the seventeenth century though, slaves from West Africa had become the standard workforce in the Americas and the Caribbean. Once again, this proved to be a matter of brute economics, rather than any subtler motivation. One black writer has summed up the financial implication of the two competing systems in this way; 'A white servant's services for ten years amounted to the price of a Negro slave. Three Negroes worked better than and cost as much as one white man' (Williams, 1970).

In the face of such remorseless logic, there was little to be done, other than to phase out indentured servitude in favour of black slavery. One powerful incentive for the expansion of slavery in this form was that it greatly increased the profits of the owners of ships trading with the New World. Thus, economic expediency, rather than racism or colonialism, was the driving force behind the transatlantic slave trade. To understand this, we need to think about the nature of trade at that time.

Merchant ships typically sailed to another part of the world either to collect some valuable commodity or to transport to that place something which could be sold there. This meant that often the ships sailed either there or back with empty holds, and that part of the voyage would bring in no profit for the owners of the ship. Once the so-called Triangular Trade had become established, this wasted time had been altogether eliminated. At every stage of the voyage, the ship would be carrying valuable goods; manufactured items to Africa, slaves to America and sugar to Britain.

As was remarked above, the actual capture of slaves formed no part of the white people's work. This was done for them by black rulers. Slavery was an accepted way of life in West Africa and while it may have been stimulated by the coming of Europeans, they certainly did not introduce slavery to the coast of Africa. Of course, once it became apparent to those running the societies which existed in that part of the continent where the countries of Nigeria and Ghana are today that there was an unlimited market for slaves, they did not hesitate to put all their efforts into satisfying that demand. This resulted in wide-ranging expeditions into the interior in search of tribes whom they might conquer and then bring to the ports of their kingdoms so that they could be bartered for firearms and gunpowder. With such new armament, they were enabled to subdue even more districts and so a vicious circle was established whereby supply and demand both rose inexorably.

The influence of European slave traders in this matter was wholly baleful for all concerned. Even if one of the kings or chiefs in West Africa had been minded to avoid becoming involved, his refusal to participate in the business would very likely cost him dear. Firearms and gunpowder meant power. They were the means to maintain independence and fight off enemies who might only be carrying spears. Refusing to trade with the Europeans, bartering slaves for guns, would in effect mean that such a leader would find that a neighbouring chief with fewer scruples would end up being equipped with muskets, while he was compelled to make do with bows and arrows or spears. In such a case, it would be only a matter of time before the group armed with firearms would launch an attack on his more principled neighbour, who might very well find that he and his people were taken as prisoners of war and so sold to the traders who would ship them off to another continent as slaves. There was thus every incentive for rulers to come to accommodations with the white slave traders and no reason to refrain from doing so. It was simply a matter of survival.

There can be no doubt that the transatlantic slave trade was a cruel and bloody business. Most estimates suggest that over the course of 350 years, between 10 and 12 million black people were taken forcibly from their homes in West Africa and carried across the Atlantic. The sheer magnitude of this appalling enterprise, however, sometimes discourages anybody from asking searching questions about who was responsible for the thing. At the time of writing this is a very 'hot' topic, especially in the wake of the Black Lives Matter protests which were seen in Britain and the United States in the summer of 2020.

Statues of those who were supposed by protestors to be involved in this particular slave trade were defaced or pulled down. In Britain, such a statue in the port of Bristol, once an important city in the transatlantic slave trade, was toppled and then thrown in the harbour. Nobody at that time wished to be reminded of the part which black Africans themselves played in the slave trade, all the blame being heaped solely and exclusively upon white people. There were those though who raised their eyebrows at this enthusiasm for the destruction of statues and they wondered why it did not extend to Africa itself.

There is a square in the former Nigerian capital Lagos which is named after a woman called Efunroye Tinubu. A statue of her stands in the town of Abeokuta. This statue is interesting, because it commemorates a nineteenth-century Yoruba woman who was something of a kingmaker. She is very famous in Nigeria, not least for the fact that much of her wealth came from the slave trade. This was not in the modern sense, that perhaps her great grandfather had owned shares in a company which had commercial interests in the Caribbean, but rather that she herself bought and sold slaves and by doing so made a fortune. This is such a curious story that it might be worth relating it here. Before doing so, we must observe that at no time have any Nigerians ever appeared to be ashamed of or embarrassed about the statue of this slave trader. On the contrary, they are proud of her.

Efunroye Tinubu was born into a Yoruba family in what is now Nigeria in 1810. Her father was a merchant and his daughter followed in his footsteps, specializing in the buying and selling of salt, tobacco and slaves (Yemitan, 1987). She married several times, one of her husbands being an Oba or king who was in exile. Tinubu managed to restore him to his throne in Lagos, but then when he died, found herself forced into exile. She continued to trade in slaves and also branched out into gunrunning.

In 1851 the British navy shelled Lagos as part of their efforts to stamp out slavery in Africa. The following year, a formal treaty was signed in which the kings and chiefs of Nigeria agreed that they would no longer tolerate the practice in areas under their control. There was a great reluctance on the part of many people in this part of Africa to give up what they regarded as a time-honoured and traditional occupation. Efunroye Tinubu was one of those who felt that the treaty was an infringement on her rights. She was challenged about this and mounted a spirited defence of her actions.

> On one occasion, during her final sojourn in Abeokuta, she was alleged to have sold a young boy into slavery and was accused of it. When arraigned before Ogundipe Alatise over the matter, she reportedly explained: 'I have a large household and I must feed them well. I need money to do that, that's why.' (Yemitan, 1987)

On another occasion, Tinubu was told that she really had to free all the remaining slaves in her possession. Instead, she tried to sell them to a trader called Domingo Martinez. When she felt that he was trying to cheat her she said, and nobody doubted her word, that she would sooner drown the twenty men and women whom she was haggling about than sell them at too low a price (Yemitan, 1987).

We have to some degree anticipated the theme of a later chapter here, in that it has been shown how the practice of slavery and the trade in captive humans was flourishing among Africans in the nineteenth century. In fact, they many of them felt indignant at the idea of being forced to free slaves and to stop buying and selling them in the future. Efunroye Tinubu is regarded in Nigeria as something of a heroine for her resistance to British influence and this led to a statue being erected to her in the town of Abeokuta, where she spent a large part of her life. It is amusing to note that with all the fuss about statues in Britain with links to the slave trade, nobody in Nigeria seems in the least inclined to deface Tinubu's statue. That she traded in slaves is common knowledge, but it has not diminished her standing in the modern country.

It was in the seventeenth century that the slave trade between West Africa and the Americas really took off. Portugal had of course established an early grip on that part of Africa and although there had been the odd British expedition to find slaves, it was hardly big business. Francis Drake, for instance, was mixed up in a little slave trading in the sixteenth century. It was a European country which is today a byword for its liberal and progressive ways which precipitated something akin to a gold rush for African slaves. The Dutch had always been aggressive traders and once they had thrown off the Spanish forces occupying their country, as they did in 1581, the Dutch turned their eyes to international trade, which included what they could see was a most profitable business; that of slaves. After founding various colonies in what became known as the East Indies, the islands which lay between Australia and Asia, they turned their attention to the Americas and the Caribbean.

We sometimes forget just what a ferociously expansionist nation the Dutch were during the seventeenth century and how they were responsible for the enormous growth of the trade in slaves from West Africa. In 1621 the Dutch West India Company was founded and five years later, a stronghold was established in North America, with the building of a fort which became the town of New Amsterdam. This, in the course of time and after being captured by the British, became New York. In 1630, a large chunk of Brazil was taken from the Portuguese and the Dutch also broke the virtual monopoly on slave trading which the Portuguese had until then enjoyed in West Africa. Seeing Portuguese dominance fading, the British were swift to take advantage and stake claims of their own along that part of the African coast. This was of course done with the aim of taking their own share of slaves and transporting them to the plantations of the Caribbean.

The various European nations were competing with each other and obtained permission from local kings to build forts and stockades, where they could keep the slaves which they had acquired until a ship should be ready to take them across the Atlantic. It would be impossible readily to distinguish at this time between colonialism, in the sense of a country staking a claim to territory in some part of the world, and commercial exploitation for the sake of profit. In England there was a company, for instance, which effectively ran India. This was the East India Company. Was this colonialism or was it simply private enterprise? Similarly, there were in West Africa forts erected and treaties signed with African kings which looked as though they were agreements between sovereign nations. Of course, where the merchants managed to get a toehold, the British government would in later years often take over from them and regularise the position by adding this or that territory to the British Empire. So it was that in the nineteenth century, Britain simply took over the management of India from the East India Company, transforming Queen Victoria into the Empress of India in the process.

In the exploitation of Africans by Europeans which was taking place in the seventeenth century, the advantage was now all in one direction. There was a constant struggle between the representatives of the companies which were operating the day-to-day running of affairs in Africa and the kings with whom they dealt. Not to put too fine a point on it, each side was doing its best to cheat the other. The factors, the name for the company representatives, were not always men of the highest moral and intellectual calibre. The agent-general of a French concern on the Gold Coast wrote scathingly about the factors whom he encountered, in terms which we would perhaps today hesitate to use.

> They are mainly men of no education or principles, void of foresight, careless, prodigal, addicted to strong liquors and overfond of the black women whose natural hot and lewd temper soon wastes their bodies and consumes what little substance they have. (Barbot, 1999)

It was the factors who had to negotiate licences to trade and come to agreement on how many Europeans would be able to live on the coast. In addition to these two main players, the rulers and the factors, there were also interpreters and various hangers-on, all of whom were trying to make money on their own account. Some of these people were black and others white. This was not a straightforward case of colonialism, when some overseas territory is occupied by a foreign power and claimed as its own. All parties in the transatlantic slave trade had their own interests at heart and there was little distinction according to the colour of their skins. The chiefs and kings of places like Benin were quite at home trading in slaves and murdering them as the mood took them as human sacrifices. It was this casual acceptance of slavery as a way of life which ensured that the Europeans would feel that here were men with whom they could do business. There was little to choose between black men and white when it came to cruelty and lack of humanity for their fellow beings.

How did the Europeans become aware that those ruling the kingdoms of West Africa with which they came into contact were likely to be sympathetic to their desire to buy slaves? Simply because as soon as they landed and looked around them, they were able to see that slaves were an integral part of the social order in the African realms which they visited. Take Benin, for example, which was a kingdom on the coast and lay where modern-day Nigeria is to be found.

The first European visitors to Benin were Portuguese. As we saw in an earlier chapter, the Portuguese were at the end of the fifteenth century making their way south, following the African coast in the hope that they would ultimately be able to find a sea passage to India. In 1485 an expedition led by Joao Afonso de Averio landed at Benin and found a city which was full of all kinds of things which their patrons in Portugal might wish to acquire; ivory, pepper, palm oil and slaves (Oliver, 1977). That it might be possible to obtain slaves from Benin was indicated by their obvious presence in the city. The Oba, or king, of the city was, 'so heavily sheathed in polished gold that when he rose to his feet he had to be propped up by two slaves' (Pope-Hennessy, 1967).

The presence of slaves was simply taken for granted by those who visited kingdoms like Benin and we shall be seeing a lot more of this African attachment to slavery in later chapters. It is time now to look at how both the transatlantic slave trade and also that carried out by the states of North Africa both came to an end in the early part of the nineteenth century. It might have been thought that once the slave trade from West and North Africa was over, then this would pretty well mean the end of slavery and slave trading in Africa, but nothing could be further from the truth.

Chapter 8

The Abolition of the British Slave Trade and the End of the Barbary Pirates

Anybody living in Britain in the middle of the eighteenth century might have been forgiven for assuming that slavery, that is to say the transatlantic slave trade and the unpaid black workers on plantations in the Caribbean and North America, was a fact of life and likely to remain so forever. After all, Britain had done well out of slavery and there was, on the face of it, no incentive for anybody to meddle with, still less to dismantle, the institution. A large part of the nation's prosperity seemed to be founded upon slavery in the colonies and as the Industrial Revolution gathered pace it must have seemed a bad idea to try any experiment which might radically alter the basis of British economic success. Any such move might improve matters, but so well was the British economy doing, it must have seemed equally likely that changing such a profitable part of it might harm, rather than improve, the nation's interests.

Of course, there had always been a few cranks, chiefly religious ones like Quakers, who had disapproved of slavery, but these people had only ever been a tiny and unrepresentative minority. The average person in Britain was glad to have cheap sugar and all the other benefits of slavery, especially since all the unsavoury aspects of the business took place thousands of miles away and they did not have to see the thing in practice. The British abolitionists of the seventeenth and early eighteenth centuries based their arguments on moral and ethical grounds; that it was *wrong* for human beings to be traded and owned like cattle. It is true that such a case may indeed be made and it was without doubt well-founded upon one interpretation of the

Bible. However, framing the debate in this way had two effects. First, the Biblical position on slavery and the trade in slaves is by no means straightforward and clear. There is certainly no outright condemnation of slavery to be found in either the Hebrew or Christian scriptures. Some interpretations of Christianity appear to demonstrate through close examination of scripture that slavery is divinely sanctioned and that in keeping the so-called Children of Ham in servitude as hewers of wood and carriers of water, good Christians were doing no more than obeying the will of God. Secondly, of course, none of this was of any particular interest to a hard-headed businessman who wasn't religious and cared nothing for the state of his soul. Such men could afford to disregard theological debates, whether about the number of angels who could dance on the head of a pin or whether the Deity hated or approved of the institution of slavery.

For the average British citizen, the man or woman in the street who actually benefitted, however indirectly, from the increasing wealth of the country, none of this mattered. It was enough that their lives were improving, however slightly, and they had no desire to embark upon any dangerous experiments which might damage their own interests. That sugar was no longer a luxury item but could now be afforded by all was of far more interest than the supposed suffering of Africans in the Caribbean.

So it was that the various famous court cases which took place in London relating to slavery were of only academic interest to most people in the country, either rich or poor, workers or bosses. In 1765, for instance, there was the notorious case of Johnathon Strong, a black slave who had managed to escape from his master's brutal treatment and make a life for himself in London. After two years of freedom, his supposed owner kidnapped him and sold him to a West Indian plantation owner. A few years later, in 1772, came the famous Somerset case. As with the hearing about Johnathon Strong, this concerned a black slave in Britain whose 'owner' hoped to ship him back to the Caribbean.

The same person passed judgement in the case of the slave James Somersett as decided the matter of Johnathon Strong. Lord Justice Mansfield was desperately anxious to avoid any confrontation with the rich merchants and plantation owners, men whose activities were driving the rise of Britain as a world power, but try as he might, he was forced to come down on one side of the fence or the other. In the earlier case, he had managed to avoid stating a firm view on the law relating to slavery and whether it was actually permitted in England. Expressing his relief, Mansfield said,

> I hope it will never be finally discussed, for I would have all the masters think them free, and all negroes think they were not, because then they would both behave better. (Everett, 1996)

When the case of James Somersett reached court on Friday, 7 February 1772, Lord Mansfield could no longer dodge the issue and he ruled that no law in England supported the existence of slavery.

All this was very interesting and gave a certain boost to those campaigning for the abolition of slavery in British possessions throughout the world, but four years after the Somersett case a book was published which really sounded the death-knell for the business, although it would take another few decades for the full implications of what had been written fully to sink in.

Adam Smith's *The Wealth of Nations* is one of those seminal works of which everybody has heard but which, like Darwin's *The Origin of Species*, hardly anybody has actually *read*. All that the average person knows of such books is that they were enormously influential and that an educated person *should* have read them both. Smith's *An Inquiry into the Nature and Causes of the Wealth of Nations*, to give it its full title, set out to understand the economics of the Industrial Revolution, which was changing the face of Europe. The author had very strong and decided views on the subject of slavery; views which were untouched by either sentimentality or religious scruples. After reviewing slavery in ancient Rome, Smith observed that:

> The experience of all ages and nations, I believe, demonstrates that the work done by slaves, though it appears to cost only their maintenance, is in the end the dearest of any. A person who can acquire no property, can have no other interest but to eat as much, and to labour as little as possible. Whatever work he does beyond what is sufficient to purchase his own maintenance can be squeezed out of him by violence only, and not by any interest of his own. (Smith, 1776)

Adam Smith's main point was an obvious one, that slaves have no possible reason to work hard, other than the constant threat of violence. They will always seek to do as little work as they can get away with and will never try and find ways to produce more or look for more efficient means of working. Their only aim is to do the absolute bare minimum that will protect them from punishment for idleness. This is very different from the free worker, who might be paid more if he works harder, or even be promoted if he comes up with a new and better way of undertaking some activity or process. There is a motive for doing the best that they can, because then perhaps they will manage to earn more money and save enough so that they are able to buy a house or provide for a family. None of this is applicable to slaves, who will never be able to improve their lot.

There was a natural corollary to this and it was one of supreme importance at a time that steam engines and labour-saving machinery were transforming the means of production in Britain and ultimately the world. Just as slaves had no reason to work harder than necessary or find ways to improve the efficiency of their labour, so too did their owners feel no need to seek innovation or investigate different methods of harvesting crops or manufacturing goods. When there is a plentiful supply of labour in which you have already invested your capital, there is no point in devising new machinery or finding ways of using waterwheels or steam engines to do the heavy work. Just use more manpower and the problem is solved. In this way, slavery acts to discourage and prevent progress, keeping a society at a primitive and pre-industrial level. This was hardly a desirable state of affairs, although it had never occurred to most people to think of it as clearly as Smith.

Consider the case of two farms or plantations, one using paid workers and the other with a labour force of slaves. If you have a hundred slaves and the going gets hard with some task upon which ten or twenty of them are engaged, whether planting, harvesting or digging ditches, then the solution is obvious. You call in more of your slaves to get the work done. Now let us think about a man running a similar farm and using free workers who all have to be paid. If you find that twenty men cannot complete some task or other, then hiring another twenty men and paying their wages is likely to cut into any future profits. What though if you can devise a piece of machinery which enables not twenty or forty men to harvest a field of crops, but just two or three? It is this process which led ultimately to the modern situation, whereby one man driving a combine harvester can undertake the work of fifty or more men working in the fields with scythes. Slavery, in this instance, has had the effect of stifling innovation and progress. Smith was shown to be a true prophet almost a century after the publication of *The Wealth of Nations*, when the American Civil War took place. The largely agrarian southern states, whose economies were wholly dependent upon slavery, proved to be no match for the heavily industrialized northern states.

According to Adam Smith, the primary reason that slavery existed, and that there was reluctance to its abolition, was psychological rather than economic.

> The pride of man makes him love to domineer, and nothing
> mortifies him so much as to be obliged to condescend to

(Right): 1. Pope Gregory and the English slaves in Rome.

(Below): 2. Black African slave traders with some of their captives.

(Left): 3. Olaudah Equiano was captured and sold into slavery by black African slave traders.

(Below): 4. The Hebrews as slaves in ancient Egypt, according to the nineteenth-century view.

(*Above left*): 5. Statue of a Nubian slave from ancient Egypt.

(*Above right*): 6. Garamantes chariot of the kind used for hunting slaves in Africa over 2,000 years ago.

7. Young women from what is now Ethiopia being carried into slavery by Arabs.

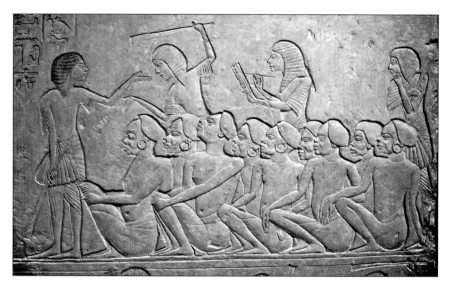

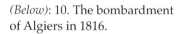

(*Above*): 8. Nubian slaves in ancient Egypt. (Mike Knell)

(*Left*): 9. The Berlin Conference of 1884.

(*Below*): 10. The bombardment of Algiers in 1816.

11. European slaves in North Africa in the early part of the nineteenth century.

(*Above left*): 12. White Circassian slave with his Arab owner.

(*Above right*): 13. The last moments of Gordon of Khartoum; an iconic image from Victorian Britain.

14. A slave market in Zanzibar during the nineteenth century.

15. A slave caravan in East Africa in the nineteenth century.

(*Above*): 16. British
sailors with freed
African slaves.

(*Right*): 17.
British armed
forces bombard
a stronghold of
slavers in East
Africa in the late
nineteenth century.

18. Barbary pirates in action.

19. Barbary pirates.

20. Slaves working a water wheel in nineteenth-century Egypt.

persuade his inferiors. Wherever the law allows it, and the nature of the work can afford it, therefore, he will generally prefer the service of slaves to that of freemen. (Smith, 1776)

By giving examples of places where slavery had been abandoned and replaced by the hiring of free workers, Smith showed that slavery was really holding back the growth of the economy in the British Empire. It took time, but nobody could ignore the arguments set forth on this subject in the greatest book on economics every written.

It was to be over 30 years after the publication of *The Wealth of Nations* that the British finally outlawed the slave trade throughout the whole of the British Empire. There was certainly much opposition to this move, not least from Africa, where many chiefs and kings were horrified to find that their principal means of making money had suddenly been declared a criminal activity. As we have seen, there was slavery and slave trading in Africa long before the Europeans came, but in the centuries since the Portuguese had first shown an interest in buying slaves in West Africa, the economies of a number of territories in that part of Africa had become heavily dependent on the slave trade and African leaders simply could not understand why the British of all people had chosen not to buy any more slaves.

One African leader who was most put out by the unilateral decision of the British to withdraw from the slave trade was the King of Bonny, a coastal territory in the Igbo-speaking part of what is today Nigeria. Bonny had profited greatly from the slave trade, by raiding in the interior and seizing villagers from those districts which had no warriors strong enough to resist them. Since the soldiers and slavers of Bonny were equipped with up-to-date European muskets, they were usually more than a match for anybody in neighbouring countries. The King of Bonny was aghast to be informed that all this had now to come to an end. He said,

We think this trade must go on. That is the verdict of our oracle and the priests. They say that your country, however

great, can never stop a trade ordained by God himself.
(Oluwatayo–Adeuyan, 2011)

Other Africans were equally dismayed at this high-handed behaviour
on the part of the British, for many years their best customers. To
begin with, other countries were still in the market for slaves and so the
Portuguese continued to ship slaves to Brazil and the Spanish wanted
them for estates in Cuba, but the British were not minded to allow
anybody to gain any sort of advantage over them for what they hoped
would be seen as a noble and high-minded action. They began putting
pressure on both the Africans and also European nations in an effort
to prevent any slave trade taking place anywhere in Africa. During
the nineteenth century, this determination acquired the character of
a crusade, with the Royal Navy patrolling the seas around both West
and East Africa in an attempt to prevent any slaving in the continent.

We shall explore at some length the consequences of the British
decision not only to abolish their own slave trade but to take vigorous
steps to stamp out the trade of other countries in the next chapter. For
now though, we turn north to see what was happening as regards the
trade in slaves which had been flourishing in the Muslim countries on
the Mediterranean coast of Africa.

The British had of course, as we have seen, proved that they could,
if they felt it necessary, subdue by force of arms any of the states such
as Algiers, Tunis or Tripoli. It was absurd that such backward little
statelets should still be operating as corsairs and slavers during the
Industrial Revolution, especially as the targets for their depredations
were some of the most sophisticated countries in the world at that
time, the nations of Europe. How the trade in slaves, at least those
of white European origin, finally came to an end in North Africa is a
fascinating story and beautiful example of *realpolitik* in action.

Had they wished to launch a prolonged and expensive war against
the Ottoman Empire, which was, in theory at least, the ruler of North
Africa, it is possible that the British navy could have suppressed the

activities of the corsairs once and for all in the eighteenth century. This would though have been a tremendously costly enterprise, with an outcome which was far from certain. Besides which, although they were something of a nuisance to Britain, the Barbary States caused even more problems for countries like Spain, which was much closer to North Africa than Britain.

At about the time that serious suggestions were being made in Britain that slavery should be brought to an end in Africa and across the British Empire, the trade in white slaves in North Africa began coming to an end. This did not happen overnight of course, any more than the end of the British trade in slaves did, but in retrospect it may be seen that the Barbary pirates would not still be plying their trade in the nineteenth century as they had been doing in the eighteenth. Curiously enough, it was the last country which anybody would have expected to become involved in the business which took the decisive action necessary to deal a mortal blow to the Barbary pirates.

As will be recalled from an earlier chapter, Britain had reached a *modus vivendi* with the states of North Africa, one which was agreeable all parties. This entailed paying annual tribute in order for British merchant vessels to be left alone in the Mediterranean and along the Atlantic coast of Africa, where some of the slavers also operated. Ships sailing to and from America were included in this immunity, as the American colonies were part of Britain's empire.

Readers might perhaps be a little surprised that as the end of the eighteenth century drew nigh, slavers were still sailing from Algiers, Tunis and so on. It might have been thought that the massive defeats inflicted on city-states such as Algiers by the British and French would have been enough to signal a final end to the seizure of ships in the Mediterranean and the taking of their crews into slavery. It did have the effect of stopping such activity for a while, but then there was a stroke of luck for the Barbary pirates. As long as any of the European countries was able to give the matter their undivided attention and to muster a fleet, then no city like Tunis or Tripoli would be able to withstand the bombardment of modern artillery which must result from such a concerted action. Fortunately though, just as things were getting a little uncomfortable for the corsairs, Europe slipped once more into generalized warfare, in which most nations joined. For some people in North Africa, this was an opportunity too good to miss.

Five years after Spain launched a great bombardment against Algiers in 1784, in retaliation for the seizure of their ships, the French Revolution took place. Because the King of France's wife happened to be the sister of Leopold II, the Holy Roman Emperor, this meant that the revolution, which of course featured the deposing and execution of the king and his wife, was unlikely to remain a purely domestic affair involving only the French. Leopold rallied various European countries and they declared war on the revolutionary regime in France. First Austria and Prussia and then Spain and Portugal fought against the new republican government. These French Revolutionary Wars segued seamlessly into the Napoleonic Wars, once Bonaparte had seized power in France, and the fighting spread across the entire world, from Scandinavia in the north to Southern Africa in the south and from Moscow and the Middle East to the West Indies. While Europe tore itself apart, the corsairs of the Barbary Coast thought this might allow them to resume their traditional occupation without any interference on the part of the European powers.

Something else happened during the 1780s of course, although it was a long way from Africa and the Mediterranean. Britain's American colonies broke free and declared their independence. This was very embarrassing for the British and once it was plain that there was no chance of regaining these territories, Britain did all that they could to make life difficult for the new nation. One of the things they did was to inform the Barbary States that ships flying the American flag were no longer under British protection and that if anybody wished to attack or harass such shipping, then this was nothing to do with Britain. This was more than mere malice or spite. As a mercantile nation, the British were not at all keen to see another country bringing desirable produce and goods to sell in Europe. There was, for example, a great demand in Europe for tobacco and the newly formed United States had plenty of that to sell.

The British and Americans both knew perfectly well that encouraging the slavers to attack American shipping would be a sound policy on Britain's part. In 1783, the year that the war between Britain and America officially ended, a book written by the Earl of Sheffield was published in London. Although the title was long-winded, the observations which it contained were exceedingly shrewd. *Observations on the commerce of the American states with Europe and the West Indies: including the several articles of import and export, and on the tendency of a bill now depending in Parliament* contained a statement which was at that time perfectly true, 'The Americans cannot protect themselves as they cannot pretend to have a navy' (Holroyd, 1783). This was a reasonable point, because for all that the British found it convenient to pay tribute each year, they were also well able to launch a punitive expedition against any part of North Africa should the occasions arise. The newly independent United States, on the other hand, had no warships and were thousands of miles from the Mediterranean.

In the same year that the Earl of Sheffield's book was published, Benjamin Franklin was in France as the United States ambassador to that country. He was hoping to arrange for the purchase by the United States of machinery and other manufactured goods which would be bought in Europe and then shipped to America via the Mediterranean port of Trieste. This was of vital importance to the new country, for if they wished to become a modern, industrialized nation, it was clear that to begin with they would need to import many of the things which they were unable at that time to make themselves.

Talking of the hazards of trying to ship cargoes through the Mediterranean and North Atlantic, Benjamin Franklin wrote the following:

> I think it not improbable that those rovers may be privately encouraged by the English to fall upon us, and to prevent our interference in the carrying trade; for I have heard in

London that it is a maxim among the merchants there that *if
there were no Algiers it would be worth England's while to build
one.* (Wharton, 1888)

Nobody had any doubt at the time that Britain believed that they
could use the corsairs of North Africa to their own advantage, both
by punishing the confederation of colonies which had defeated them
so humiliatingly and also by spiking the guns of what might grow to
be a serious commercial rival in European trade.

At the time that America broke free of Britain's control, they had
only a few small vessels for patrolling the coast and the last thing on the
mind of any of the revolution's leaders was building a navy which would
fight off the coast of Europe or Africa. They had enough to occupy their
minds in consolidating their position on the domestic front, without
troubling themselves about any foreign adventures. Even so, if the
United States was to survive then it would be necessary to export their
goods to Europe and also to import machinery and other manufactured
goods which they were not yet able to produce themselves. The freedom
of their ships on the high seas was of great importance.

It did not take the slavers of North Africa long to realize that
American ships were fair game. In 1784, the year following the end
of the American Revolutionary War, an American merchantman was
boarded in the Atlantic by corsairs operating from Morocco and the
crew taken as slaves. There was then a fierce debate among the leaders
of the revolution such as Thomas Jefferson and James Monroe as to
the best way to proceed. Jefferson was in favour of prompt military
action to discourage further attacks on shipping, but others thought
that it might be better policy to enter into the same kind of financial
arrangements as those which European nations had negotiated.

It might at this point be helpful to consider in general the likely
course of events when money is demanded under the threat of violence
or other unpleasant consequences. History teaches us that whether
the requests for payment are being made by individuals or sovereign

nations, the essential nature of the transaction remains the same; that is to say giving way to the threat will be followed by further demands for money and these will often be for greater amounts than the original sum. This general principle holds true for the personal blackmailer and aggressive nation alike. Rudyard Kipling summed up the situation in his poem *Dane-Geld*.

There was a time in England, before the Norman Conquest of 1066, when Danish forces who behaved very much like pirates arrived in the country and threatened to wreak havoc unless they were given gold to go away. This payment, very similar to the 'tribute' paid by Britain and other countries to the Barbary States, was known as the Dane-Geld. It will surprise nobody to learn that the Danes returned whenever they felt like it and repeated the extortion. In the same way, it is to be doubted that many readers will be shocked by the fact that their greed increased with every payment. As Kipling wrote,

> And that is called paying the Dane-Geld:
> But we've proved it again and again,
> That if once you have paid him the Dane-Geld
> You never get rid of the Dane.
> (Kipling, 1911)

In the years following the achievement of independence, money was fairly tight for the government of the United States and it seemed on the face of it more economical to make a substantial payment to Morocco to avoid having any more ships intercepted as they sailed across the North Atlantic. After all, this was what Britain and the other countries in Europe were doing and it would certainly be cheaper than building a navy with the ability to fight battles thousands of miles away on the other side of the world. And so it was decided to pay tribute of $80,000 to Morocco and enter into a formal treaty with the country.

Events now unfolded all the inevitability of a Greek tragedy. The payment to Morocco was an unmistakable and unambiguous signal to other parts of North Africa that there was money to be made from America. In Algiers, it was thought that if a new source of income was available then it would be remiss of them not to stake their own claim. On 25 July 1785 corsairs from Algiers boarded and captured the American schooner *Maria*. A week later, the *Dauphin* was also captured and both ships were taken to Algiers where the crew were enslaved. Just as might reasonably have been foreseen, capitulating to the demands of Morocco had done nothing except stimulate interest in the United States as a profitable source of revenue.

So far, nothing which happened in the closing years of the eighteenth century in the seas around North Africa would have given anybody cause to think that a new situation was about to arise, one with consequences which echo down to the present day. After their ships were seized and taken to Algiers, the ruler there declared war on the United States and thus signalled his intention of capturing more American ships if possible and seeing their crews end up for sale in the slave markets. Once again, Kipling summed up not only the probable course of events when an international protection racket of this kind is being operated, but also the only sure answer when one country tries to obtain 'tribute', Dane-Geld or any other kind of reward for abstaining from bad behaviour. He ended his poem with the following lines:

> So when you are requested to pay up or be molested,
> You will find it better policy to say: –
> 'We never pay *any*-one Dane-Geld,
> No matter how trifling the cost,
> For the end of that game is oppression and shame,
> And the nation that plays it is lost!'
> (Kipling, 1911)

Nor were America's problems limited to Morocco and Algiers. The revolutionary regime in France tried to enlist America as an ally against the British, but this offer was firmly declined. The French were infuriated by this and so tried to exact tribute of their own from the country, by permitting their own privateers to harass American shipping. France offered a deal whereby the United States would make a one-off payment of $50,000 to the French Republic and also a loan of $10,000,000. At the same time, Algiers was attacking more American ships and selling their crews as slaves. Tunis and Tripoli meanwhile threatened attacks and persuaded the Americans to pay them tribute to have their ships left unmolested in the Mediterranean.

After a little more than a decade of these difficulties, those running the United States saw that they could no longer play the game of paying tribute. In 1796 Algiers and America finally reached a settlement. The United States would pay Algiers the enormous sum of $642,000 and thereafter $21,000 every year. In return, the sailors who had been sold into slavery would be freed and permitted to return home. It is possible to gauge something of the conditions under which the slaves in North Africa lived and worked when we learn that of the 131 healthy and active men who had been taken as prisoners between 1785 and 1796, no fewer than a third had died from the results of starvation or ill-treatment. Just eighty-five of the crew members taken by the corsairs remained alive (Elleman, Rosenberg and Forbes, 2010).

George Washington was of course the first president of the United States and he remained in office until 1797, when he was succeeded by John Adams. By that time, the American government had authorized payments to Morocco, Algiers, Tunis and Tripoli totalling $1.25 million (Fremont-Barnes, 2006). Since the entire annual budget of the United States that year amounted to just $6 million, it was plain that matters could not continue in that way indefinitely.

It was the Bashaw of Tripoli, which was the title of the man who ruled what was still nominally a province of the Ottoman Empire, who brought matters to a head. He became a little too greedy and began to insist that the Americans were not paying enough each year to have their ships left alone. The other parts of the Barbary Coast watched with interest to see if there was any chance that they too could rack up their demands. On 10 May 1801, Tripoli declared war on America. The Bashaw was already holding some Swedish citizens and that same year he also declared war on Sweden.

There could hardly have been a worse miscalculation on the part of the Bashaw of Tripoli. Two months before his declaration of war, a new president had taken office in America. This was Thomas Jefferson and he had for the last 17 years been urging that the policy of appeasement, for that is what the paying of tribute amounted to, was a bad one for America. As early as 1784 he had written:

> The question is whether their peace or war will be cheapest? But is it a question which should be addressed to our Honor as well as our Avarice? Nor does it respect us as to these pyrates only, but as to the nations of Europe. If we wish our commerce to be free and uninsulated, we must let these nations see that we have an energy which at present they disbelieve. The low opinion they entertain of our powers cannot fail to involve us soon in a naval war. (Boyd, Bryan and Hutter, 1953)

Now that he was president, Jefferson's view had hardened even more on the question and he asserted warmly that if America were ever to be respected in the world, then it was time to stop hesitating and to take decisive action. It was now that he used the phrase by which he is still remembered to this day; 'Millions for defence, but not one cent for tribute'.

News in those days travelled very slowly and word of the Bashaw of Tripoli's declaration of war had not yet reached Washington when a Cabinet meeting was held on 15 May 1801 at which it was agreed to send a task force to protect American shipping in the Mediterranean. Although he may not have known that the United States was technically at war, President Jefferson knew that a crisis was approaching in that part of the world and he was no longer prepared for his country to be treated with the contempt which had so far been shown towards it. He saw clearly that if America was to be respected in its dealings with European nations, then it was time to show everybody that it was a force to be reckoned with.

Now that he was in the White House, Jefferson ensured that things moved very rapidly. Just two weeks after the Cabinet meeting at which the decision had been taken to send warships to the Mediterranean, three frigates and a schooner left the harbour at Hampton Roads, which lay between Virginia and North Carolina. These four vessels represented two-thirds of the newly-formed United States Navy and the orders carried by Captain Richard Dale, the commander of the expedition, were quite explicit. He was to arrange his forces on arriving in the Mediterranean, 'So as best to protect our commerce & chastise their insolence – by sinking, burning or destroying their ships & vessels wherever you shall find them' (Swanson, 1939). There was great consternation in Tripoli when four-heavily armed American warships appeared in the Mediterranean. It must have been immediately apparent to the Bashaw that he had overplayed his hand. It only needed one encounter to show everybody which way the wind was blowing.

Today, any mention of the USS *Enterprise* is likely to put most people in mind of the television series *Star Trek*. There have been many American ships of that name though and the first of these was the schooner which sailed as part of that first American naval expedition to leave their own territorial waters. The USS *Enterprise* had been launched in 1799. She was not a large ship, being just 84ft long, but she was well armed, with a dozen 6-pounder guns and a crew of seventy. There was also a detachment of marines on board. Hoping to catch the corsairs by surprise, the *Enterprise* was flying British colours and near the island of Malta she encountered a warship from Tripoli. The *Enterprise* was commanded by a Captain Sterret. A contemporary newspaper, the Washington-based *National Intelligencer*, reported what happened next.

On the 1st of August, the schooner Enterprize, commanded by Captain Sterret, and carrying 12 six pounders and 90 men, bound to Malta for a supply of water, fell in with a Tripolitan cruiser, being a ship of 14 six pounders, manned by 80 men. At this time the Enterprize bore British colours. Captain Sterret interrogated the commander of the Tripolitan on the object of his cruize. He replied that he came out to cruize after the Americans, and that he lamented that he had not come alongside some of them. Captain Sterret, on this reply, hoisted American, in the room of British colours; and discharged a volley of musquetry; which the Tripolitan returned by a partial broadside. – This was the commencement of a hard fought action, which commenced at 9 am and lasted for three hours.

The end result of this, America's first naval battle fought away from the continental United States, was a resounding victory against the corsair. The Americans ended up boarding her and then dismantled her masts and escorted her to Tripoli, where the ruined vessel limped into the harbour. It was a salutary lesson, the repercussions of which have not yet faded away.

Just 20 years after gaining independence, America had been able to despatch ships thousands of miles and inflict a sharp defeat on a nation which had been causing difficulties for Europe over the course of two or three centuries. This was the first time that the United States acted as the world's policeman, but it was not of course the last. The next time that we hear of an America aircraft carrier being sent to some distant trouble spot, then we may reflect that this tradition had its origins in the struggle against the North African slave trade. In the next few years, more American ships were to appear in the Mediterranean, until the Barbary States were comprehensively humbled. These military expeditions became known as the First Barbary War.

Two years after the USS *Enterprise* gave Tripoli a bloody nose, the Americans were called upon to repeat the lesson, as the Bashaw of

Tripoli seemed under the impression that having once crossed the Atlantic Ocean, the United States would have forgotten about him and that he could carry on as usual. The arrival of more American ships off the Libyan coast in 1803 disabused him of such an idea and there were several brisk encounters, in which the Americans did not always come off best. Indeed, for a time it looked as though the city-state of Tripoli might prevail. In the course of one assault the American frigate *Philadelphia* ran aground and the crew were captured by fighters from Tripoli and held as bargaining chips.

The strategy of the Bashaw of Tripoli was a simple one. He thought that if only he could fight the Americans to a standstill, then sooner or later they would feel that the game was too costly and would then retreat back to their own continent and leave him to carry on with his slave trade and extortion. Thomas Jefferson though was not a man who was prepared to give up halfway through an enterprise of that sort. Once he had put his shoulder to the wheel, he would continue to the bitter end. All else apart, Jefferson knew that the countries of Europe were watching the contest with some interest. He decided that if naval power alone could not accomplish the task, then he would be compelled to use troops on land.

In 1805 the United States appointed a former soldier called William Eaton to a new role, that of 'Naval Agent to the Barbary States'. His brief was a simple one, to bring the Bashaw of Tripoli to heel. Eaton was given a free hand in the matter and the assistance of half a dozen United States marines. In addition to this, he was provided with a large sum of money and told that he could call upon the aid of American ships which had been despatched to the Mediterranean. Eaton, who was really no more than a secret agent, had an inflated idea of his own importance and began signing his letters 'Commander in Chief' and expecting the marines to address him as 'General', although he had only ever held the rank of captain in the army. Despite this, he proved a very capable man for the job and recruited a small army of mercenaries. With these and his marines, he managed to take the Libyan town of Derna. This was accomplished with the aid of bombardment by cannon fire from American ships. It was the first time that American troops had fought an engagement outside their own continent, but it was not of course to be the last.

A bully and protection racketeer he might have been, but the Bashaw of Tripoli was no fool. He made terms with the Americans and freed all the American slaves whom he held. This episode, the storming of Derna, is of course immortalized in the first verse of the Hymn of the United States Marines,

> From the Halls of Montezuma
> To the shores of Tripoli
> We fight our country's battles
> On the land as on the sea;
> First to fight for right and freedom
> And to keep our honour clean;
> We are proud to claim the title
> Of United States Marine.

There was to be one more American naval expedition to the Mediterranean before it became clear to all those in the Barbary States that interfering with American shipping was never going to worth the trouble which it brought down upon their heads. On 3 March 1815 ten ships sailed from the United States. They were commanded by Commodore Stephen Decatur and had orders to deliver an ultimatum to the Dey of Algiers (Allen, 1905). This expedition had been prompted because the Algerians had perhaps assumed that in the 10 years which had passed since the attack on Tripoli, that the United States might perhaps have lost their appetite for foreign wars. It was a fatal miscalculation. Soon after passing Gibraltar and entering the Mediterranean, the American taskforce encountered the Algerian flagship *Meshuda*. As far as the United States was concerned, they would hold any state responsible for the actions of corsairs or pirates sailing from their ports. The *Meshuda* was captured after a brief skirmish and before reaching Algiers, a second Algerian ship had also been taken. On arrival at Algiers, Commodore Decatur presented the Dey of Algiers with a stark choice. Either he could yield up all American slaves in his territory and promise never again to attack American ships or his city would be reduced to rubble by a bombardment from the sea. On 3 July 1815 the Dey signed a treaty in which he agreed to free all the American slaves in Algiers, to pay America $10,000 compensation and never to attack any more American ships. Thus ended, at least for some considerable time, the involvement of the United States in the Mediterranean.

The capture of white slaves in the way at which we have been looking was almost at an end. With the Battle of Waterloo, fought in the same year that Commodore Decatur signed the treaty with Algiers, the Napoleonic Wars which had racked Europe came to a final end. This mean that the European powers had the leisure to turn their attention to other matters, now that they were no longer waging war upon each other. They had seen how decisively America had dealt with the Barbary States and there was some uneasiness at the involvement of the United States in the Mediterranean, operating as easily and confidently as though these waters were their natural environment. If any warships should be engaged in this way, France, Britain and Spain felt that it might as well be their own. Besides, although a century or two earlier North Africa had not appeared to be an attractive prospect for colonial adventures, the view had now changed somewhat. The British, for instance, had their eyes on Egypt.

When Napoleon was fighting in Egypt in 1798, he considered the possibility of constructing a canal which would link the Red Sea with the Mediterranean. Nothing came of this tentative idea, but in the early years of the nineteenth century Britain was increasingly interested in securing communications with India. The only sea route to India at that time was around the Cape of Good Hope, the southern tip of Africa. If a canal *could* be constructed in Egypt, it would make it very much easier to remain in contact with India. The French were becoming interested in Algiers, which had agricultural land which might be cultivated by settlers using modern, scientific methods. Meanwhile, Spain was eying Morocco, where they already had some bases. After watching the actions of the Americans, it became increasingly clear in Europe that the Barbary States would be no match for modern weaponry and the determination of industrialized nations.

It must of course be borne in mind that even if the rulers of those parts of North Africa which had made such a nuisance of themselves did decide to prevent ships leaving their ports in search of slaves, that slavery was still flourishing in Egypt, Tripoli, Tunis and the other territories of that part of Africa. Black slaves were still being brought to Egypt via trade routes in Sudan and Ethiopia, while elsewhere, the Tuaregs brought slaves across the Sahara.

The British were the first to launch an attack on North Africa with a view to asserting their authority in that part of the world. The Ottoman Empire, which theoretically still extended this far, was ailing and by the 1850s would be contemptuously described as the 'sick man' of Europe. The days when the empire was an existentialist threat to Christian Europe had long passed. This meant that the British had little fear that any action against one of the Barbary States would result in a wider war with the Ottomans. The *casus belli* chosen by the British was a simple and clear-cut one. Although the major European countries had agreements which protected their ships from the slavers, the corsairs were still attacking ships from less significant parts of southern Europe such as Sicily and Sardinia. These people were Christians though and Britain felt that this would make as good grounds as any for them to take action. In 1816 Admiral Edward Pellew, backed by a squadron of warships, visited North Africa with a list of demands for the Dey of Algiers and also the men in charge of Tripoli and Tunis. The demands were simple and unequivocal. All Christian slaves from any country who were being held in the three territories were to be freed. All activity by corsairs and pirates was also to cease at once and forever. After what they had experienced at the hands of America, those in charge at Tripoli agreed at once, as did the ruler of Tunis (Taylor, 2012). The Algerians were a little harder to persuade, but eventually they too agreed to the terms. Admiral Pellew must have felt very satisfied with himself as he sailed back to Britain. He had the signatures of the three men in charge of the most notorious ports for corsairs and the attacks on shipping would now end. It only remained for arrangements to be made for the freeing of all the Christian slaves and a new era would doubtless begin in the Mediterranean. The Dey of Algiers though had felt very humiliated by the result of the negotiations with the British. No sooner had Admiral Pellew and his ships left the Mediterranean than the Dey gave orders for the massacre of hundreds of Christian slaves. The men who were killed were Corsicans, Sardinian and Sicilian fishermen who had been captured at sea and brought to Africa. Whatever their nationality though, they were all indisputably Christians and by the terms of the agreement which Admiral Pellew had secured, all Christian slaves in Algiers were under British protection. When word of the mass killings reached Britain, the admiral was ordered to provision his ships and set off again for Algiers. If retribution were not exacted, then it would reflect terribly on Britain's reputation in Europe.

On his second mission to the Mediterranean to rein in the Barbary States, Admiral Pellew's fleet was joined by six Dutch warships. Their own merchant shipping had been attacked by corsairs sailing out of Algiers and the Dutch were as keen as the British to assert their national authority. In the new order which had emerged in the aftermath of the Napoleonic Wars, it was absurd that a minor province of the declining Ottoman Empire should be allowed to act as though it was on an equal footing with great European powers. This was not how the matter presented itself to those running Algiers though and the demands made when the British and Dutch ships anchored off Algiers, the freeing of all Christian slaves and an end to the slave raids conducted at sea by the corsairs, were peremptorily refused. The following day, 27 August 1816, the fighting began. The British and Dutch bombarded Algiers and for their part the Algerians not only returned the fire from shore-based batteries of artillery and mortars, they also sent out small boats full of men who attempted to board the British and Dutch warships (Parkinson, 1977).

For all that the British were such a great naval power, the Algerian managed to inflict a good deal of damage on their enemy. This battle may be seen in Illustration 10. The casualties were higher than those seen during conventional sea battles. In total, 128 British sailors were killed and another 700 wounded. This amounts to a casualty rate of 16 per cent killed or wounded, compared with that of 9 per cent at the Battle of Trafalgar a decade earlier (Parkinson, 1977). The object of the battle had been achieved, in that the Algerian ships were all but destroyed and the batteries on the shore were out of action. The cost had been high though and not only in human life. The British had fired no fewer than 50,000 roundshot and used up an astonishing 118 tons of gunpowder. They were now unable to engage in any further military action. However, the Dey of Algiers had no way of knowing this and so Admiral Pellew thought it worth trying a bluff. Once the battle was over, he sent the following message to the Dey.

Sir, for your atrocities at Bona on defenceless Christians, and your unbecoming disregard for the demand which I made yesterday in the name of the Prince Regent of England, the fleet under my orders has given you a signal chastisement, by the total destruction of your navy, storehouse, and arsenal, with half your batteries. As England does not war for the destruction of cities, I am unwilling to visit your personal cruelties upon the unoffending inhabitants of the country, and I therefore offer you the same terms of peace which I conveyed to you yesterday in my Sovereign's name. Without the acceptance of these terms, you can have no peace with England.

The bluff was successful and the British not only received the necessary assurances that there would be no more corsairs operating out of Algiers, but arrangements were also made for a truce so that they could go ashore and see for themselves the conditions under which the European slaves were being held. One of the sailors who went ashore was a man called Captain Croker and his accounts of the slaves they saw were used as the basis for the drawings seen in Illustration 11.

The days of the corsairs and slave raids on European ships and villages came to a halt following the bombardment of Algiers in 1816, but that did not mean that slavery ended in North Africa. Slavery had been an unremarkable way of life in that part of the world for thousands of years and all that the actions of America and Britain meant was that it would be wise to avoid taking white people into slavery. In fact, later in the nineteenth century, there was an influx of white slaves into the Ottoman Empire, some of whom ended up in Egypt and other North African countries. These were, however, Circassians, whose homeland lay in the Caucasus. Circassian women ended up in harems and the men became domestic servants. One such slave can be seen in Illustration 12 with his owner. This photograph was taken in the late nineteenth century.

Slavery in Africa in general, both above and below the Sahara, continued during the nineteenth century and will be the subject of the next chapter. For now, we may say that although the trade in European slaves ended in North Africa in 1816, that in black slaves continued and even accelerated as the nineteenth century progressed. This was simply a matter of geography. Those capturing slaves intended for the Ottoman Empire had, as a general rule, to bring them overland, across the desert or up through Sudan and into Egypt. As European influence grew in North Africa, however, slavery became less and less tolerated. In places, a prohibition was placed on the practice by the colonial powers who occupied the former Barbary States, but another, subtler, influence was also at work. This was the desire of nations like Egypt to be accepted by Europe as sophisticated, modern countries. There was an awareness that slavery rather militated against such an image and this factor became stronger as the nineteenth century progressed.

Chapter 9

The Slave Trade in East Africa during the Nineteenth Century

We have seen that for the Arabs, the quest for slaves and ivory were inextricably linked; the two trades went hand in hand for many centuries. Just because the British had been so quixotic as to abolish their own slave trade, the Arabs saw no reason at all to follow suit. Even had they been minded to make do without slaves, how was all that ivory to be transported from the interior of Africa to the coast, where it could be loaded onto ships sailing north towards the Middle East? Imagine having to *pay* for the many men needed to transport those heavy tusks for hundreds of miles! It was not to be thought of.

The transatlantic slave trade was a cooperative venture between Europeans and various native kings who sought out and captured the slaves whom they then handed over to those who intended to transport them to the Americas. By contrast, the slave trade in East Africa was almost exclusively carried out by Arabs. They may from time to time have been aided by black African chieftains, but their role was not nearly so extensive as in the better-known slave trade on the other side of the continent. Sometimes, the Arabs would encourage fighting between different tribes by lending guns to one side or the other, thus allowing historic enemies to revenge themselves on each other. Once the slaughter was over, the survivors were enslaved by the Arabs and, if they were able to endure the many hardships of the journey, ended up in the slave markets of Zanzibar (Coupland, 1938). One of these may be seen in Illustration 14.

Before examining the terrible effects of the Arab slave trade in Africa, we might ask ourselves what happened to all the slaves who were rounded up and taken to the markets of Zanzibar or towns on the border between Ethiopia and Sudan. The island of Zanzibar and certain towns on the coast of what is now Kenya and Tanzania were really staging posts, where slaves were put up for sale before being exported to the Arabian Peninsula, Egypt, Turkey or even as far away as India. Those who were taken instead to markets in Ethiopia often ended up in Egypt or other parts of North Africa. Inevitably, some of those who had been buying slaves in West Africa to take to North or South America decided to make a longer voyage and acquire their stock in East Africa instead. This entailed a much more lengthy journey around the Cape of Good Hope, but it was worthwhile to begin with, at least while British efforts to enforce their abolition of the slave trade were focused on those parts of the African coast where the transatlantic slave trade had flourished. Slavers from Brazil and the United States would simply avoid the North Atlantic and head straight for Zanzibar. Apart from these buyers, the demand for slaves was entirely in the Muslim world.

As had been the case for many years, young girls were wanted as concubines and servants. These usually ended up in the Ottoman Empire. Beautiful and light-skinned girls were considered the most desirable and these were to be found in Ethiopia and Somalia, rather than further south or west. The more delicate and light-skinned, the more attractive were such girls thought to be by the Arabs and Turks who were the buyers. Most of these girls were sold at a market on the border between Ethiopia and Sudan, rather than being taken to Zanzibar. After all, they were going to be going north anyway and it would have been pointless transporting them south to Zanzibar first. The main slave market for these young women was at a place called Gallabat and we are fortunate to have a first-hand account from a British explorer who was later involved in trying to suppress the slave trade in that part of Africa.

In 1861 Samuel White Baker, an archetypal Victorian adventurer and explorer, was in Ethiopia and wrote a vivid description of the slave market at Gallabat, which dealt exclusively in girls and young women.

> The establishments of the various slave merchants were arranged under large tents of matting, and contained many young girls of extreme beauty, ranging from nine to seventeen years of age. These lovely captives, of a rich brown tint, with delicately formed features and eyes like those of the gazelle, were natives of the Galla, on the borders of Abyssinia, from which country they were brought by Abyssinian traders to be sold for the Turkish harems. Although beautiful, these girls were useless for hard labour; they quickly fade away and die unless kindly treated. (Baker, 1867)

Baker had some success in freeing slaves, but was not able to do as much as he would have liked in that direction. Illustration 16 is of men under Baker's command freeing slaves after a caravan heading towards Egypt had been intercepted.

Healthy able-bodied men were always a marketable commodity in Egypt, other Arab countries of the Middle East, and also of course in what is now Turkey, where the rulers of the Ottoman Empire lived. These slaves were used for the heaviest, dirtiest and most backbreaking labour. Some ended up being castrated and employed as guards in harems. The main slave trade in East Africa took place in Zanzibar, which in the nineteenth century had mutated from a being a Portuguese colony to an Omani one.

As early as the beginning of the sixteenth century, Portugal had staked out a claim to Zanzibar. The Portuguese were at this time claiming various parts of the world as their own, ranging from territories in North and South America to large chunks of Africa. Their colonization of the island of Zanzibar was not without opposition though from the inhabitants, who, by and large, seemed to prefer to be part of the Muslim sphere of influence. A British ship calling at Zanzibar towards the end of the sixteenth century saw no indication of Portuguese control, although the island was supposedly being administered from Mozambique, which was definitely a Portuguese possession and would remain so until the 1970s. In the seventeenth century, the influential citizens of Zanzibar invited the Sultan of Oman to take over the country (Eliot, 1905). This process was accomplished smoothly enough, and the Portuguese conceded the administration of Zanzibar without too much fuss. It was from this time that Zanzibar became established as the major East African centre for the trade in slaves.

During the seventeenth and eighteenth centuries, there was a brisk trade in slaves in Zanzibar, but then in the first decades of the nineteenth century a situation arose which meant that Zanzibar itself also required a large body of slave labour. As the British gradually brought to an end the plantations worked by slave labour in their own possessions in the Caribbean, so at the same time this system began in Zanzibar. The crop was cloves. The clove tree originated in the Molucca islands of Indonesia and was exported from there by Asian traders first to China and then Egypt and Europe (Martin, 1991). When the Portuguese and Dutch arrived in Indonesia in the sixteenth century, both countries attempted to establish a worldwide monopoly for the market in cloves. It will be remembered that the trade in spices was one of the motivations behind the exploration and colonization which took place at this time. They succeeded pretty well in cornering the market between them, until the French obtained some seeds and began cultivating them on the island of Mauritius. At some point in the early nineteenth century, seeds from a clove tree were brought to Zanzibar and grown there. The island's climate proved to be perfect for the plant and it did not take long for the first plantation to be established, which was running by 1820. Fifteen years later, there were 4,000 clove trees growing in Zanzibar and although the Dutch still had a stranglehold on the production of cloves, Zanzibar was bidding fair to being a major producer itself, a situation which has persisted up to the present day. It was an agricultural venture which, like cotton in the United States, was entirely dependent upon the labour of black African slaves.

Estimates as to the number of black Africans who were taken from their homes in the course of the East African slave trade vary dramatically. The highest estimates are made by African historians and in his book on the subject Senegalese author Tidiane N'Diaye settles on a figure of 17 million over the course of some centuries (N'Diaye, 2008). This was, it is suggested, made up of eight million people transported north from East Africa across the Sahara Desert and another nine million who passed through the markets in Zanzibar and other slave trading ports on the coast of what are now Kenya and Tanzania. It has to be said that some historians find such figures absurdly large. Abdulazizi Lodhi, Emeritus Professor of Swahili and African Linguistics at the University of Uppsala in Sweden, points out with some justification that accurate figures are simply not available.

Reginald Coupland, an acknowledged expert on the slave trade in East Africa who between 1920 and 1948 held the Beit Professorship of Colonial History at the University of Oxford, concluded after decades of study that between 80,000 and 100,000 people in East Africa died each year during the nineteenth century as a result of the slave trade (Coupland, 1938). This figure included not only those who were taken from their homes and ended up as slaves in the Middle East or North Africa, but also the many who were massacred incidentally to the slave trade; of which, more later. David Livingstone, who was as one might say the man on the spot, in that he was actually living and working in that part of Africa when the slave trade was at its height, believed that five times as many as this were dying each year.

Having seen why the slaves were being taken and considered their ultimate destinations, we look now at why the mortality rate should have been so high for this particular type of slave trade. Part of the explanation lies in the way that the Arabs and their allies who operated the traffic in human victims succeeded in overcoming any opposition from the inhabitants of those areas which they targeted. This was done by stimulating and encouraging warfare between tribes who saw themselves as hereditary enemies. By supplying one group with guns and inciting them to attack the villages of others, the Arabs could simply stand aside and wait until half the people were slain, and then step in and take their pick of the survivors. It did not really matter to them how many people were massacred, always providing that enough were left to carry the tusks of ivory to the coast.

Sometimes, the Arabs would adopt a more subtle policy and a group would settle in some remote part of the Congo and pretend that they wished to live peacefully with the neighbouring tribes. They would even plant crops and trade honestly with those living nearby, until they became accepted as decent and respectable neighbours. Henry Drummond, a Victorian scientist and devout Christian, gave a vivid description of what would happen once the initial suspicions of the natives had been allayed.

> One day, suddenly, the inevitable quarrel is picked. And then follows a wholesale massacre. Enough only are spared from the slaughter to carry the ivory to the coast; the grass huts of the village are set on fire; the Arabs strike camp; and the slave march, worse than death, begins. (Drummond, 1889)

The object of the exercise was to obtain enough slaves initially to carry the heavy elephants' tusks to the coast, but once on the march then other people might also be captured. It did not matter in the least to the slave traders how many people would be killed in pursuit of their commercial interests. In this way, whole districts became depopulated. Henry Drummond travelled through East Africa and left a vivid, eyewitness account of the aftermath of the Arab slave trade in the late nineteenth century.

It was but yesterday that an explorer crossing from Lake Nyasa to Lake Tanganyika, saw the whole southern end of Tanganyika peopled with large and prosperous villages. The next to follow him found not a solitary human being – nothing but burned houses and bleaching skeletons. It was but yesterday – the close of 1887 – that the Arabs at the north end of Lake Nyasa, after destroying 14 villages with many of their inhabitants, pursued the population of one village into a patch of tall grass, set it on fire, surrounded it, and slew with the bullet and spear those who crawled out from the more merciful flames. (Drummond, 1889)

Having by whatever means seemed to them best, regardless of the death toll, secured what they thought was the optimum number of slaves, the Arabs then loaded them with ivory and started the march east to the ships which would take them to Zanzibar. In many ways, this was the most arduous part of the whole process and many did not make it to the coast. Illustrations 15 shows a slave caravan crossing East Africa at this time. David Livingstone wrote of one convoy of slaves which he had seen, one which consisted chiefly of children and young people, who were too small to be able to carry elephant tusks,

In less time than I take to talk about it, these unfortunate creatures – 84 of them – wended their way into the village where we were. Some of them, the eldest, were women from 20 to 22 years of age, and there were youths from 18 to 19, but the large majority was made up of boys and girls from 7 years to 14 or 15 years of age. A more terrible scene than these men, women and children, I do not think I ever came across. To say that they were emaciated would not give you an idea of what human beings can undergo under certain circumstances. Each of them had his neck in a large forked stick weighing from 30 to 40 pounds, and five or six feet long. (Seaver, 1957)

Some of the sights which David Livingstone witnessed in connection with the Arab slave trade were almost beyond belief.

> I was shown a spot in the bushes where a poor woman the day before, unable to keep on the march, and likely to hinder it, was cut down by the axe of one of these slave drivers. We went on further and were shown a place where a child lay. It had been recently born, and its mother was unable to carry it from debility and exhaustion; so the slave-trader had taken this little infant by its feet and dashed its brains out against one of the trees and thrown it in there. (Seaver, 1957)

Grim it may have been, but this trade brought wealth and prosperity to Zanzibar and some parts of the African mainland which were controlled by the Arabs of Oman. Indeed, Zanzibar was becoming such a thriving place that in 1840 the Sultan of Oman, Seyyid Said, moved his entire household from Oman to Zanzibar and declared it to be the new capital of his empire. Perhaps 'empire' is rather too grandiose a word to describe the territories ruled by the Omanis at that time. Apart from Oman and Muscat on the southern end of the Arabian Peninsula, it included Zanzibar and a few ports such as Mombasa, which the sultan had claimed a few years earlier.

It was perhaps inevitable that Omani pretensions in Africa should have led to conflict with Britain, because not only had the British outlawed slavery in their own empire, they were keen to eradicate the practice throughout the whole of Africa. This led to friction with Arab slavers because they were disinclined to abandon a most lucrative trade which, as we have seen, was bound up with the exploitation of ivory.

The British campaign against slavery in East Africa and in particular that part of the Indian Ocean that provided the routes for ships carrying slaves to the Arab world and Ottoman Empire differed in one important respect from the largely successful efforts to dismantle the transatlantic slave trade. That campaign had been conducted against white Christian nations, while the suppression of slavery in East Africa was explicitly aimed at Arabs and other Muslims. There was thus a racial and religious aspect to the business which could hardly be separated from Britain's imperial ambitions in Africa during the course of the nineteenth century. In short, it was hardly an entirely disinterested affair and provided the British with a ready-made *casus belli* against nations whose territory was a tempting target for British expansion. Kenya provides a good example of how this process worked in practice and the way in which colonialism and the crusade against slavery worked hand in hand towards the same end.

The city of Mombasa was a trading port which existed at least 1,000 years ago. Whether it was founded by black Africans or Arab merchants has been a matter of some debate, but what is indisputable is that there was extensive Arab influence in Mombasa and the other settlements along the coast facing the Indian Ocean. The oldest buildings in the city bear inscriptions in Arabic. Despite some efforts by the Portuguese to claim the area for their own, it was the Omanis who historically held greater sway. This was particularly so in the middle of the nineteenth century, after the Sultan of Oman had moved his court to Zanzibar. The British had made some attempts to take over this part of East Africa as early as the 1820s, at which time Mombasa had been declared a British protectorate. This state of affairs ended when Sultan Sayed Said annexed Mombasa as part of his empire in 1837.

The slave trade at which we have been looking flourished under Omani rule as never before, but as the century drew on and European countries staked claims during what is sometimes known as the 'scramble for Africa', it will hardly come as a surprise to learn that eyes were turned on the fertile land of Kenya, Zanzibar and what is now Tanzania. However long their association with the area, it could hardly be expected that any Arab dynasty could hope to resist the advance of the European colonists. It was really a question of which country would be first to stake its claim on that part of the East African coast.

The British navy began to make its presence felt from the 1840s. In 1847, Zanzibar and Britain signed an agreement in which the sultan agreed to stop importing slaves from Africa and to allow the Royal Navy to search Omani vessels. There was no provision for the abolition of slavery in either Zanzibar or anywhere on the coast. This would have been impractical, because a large part of Zanzibar's prosperity depended upon the clove plantations which were worked by slave labour. On the Kenyan coast, it has been estimated that over 40 per cent of the population were slaves. For the time being, the British were content to see the trade in slaves from Africa to other destinations curbed.

It is never wise to accept the judgements and evaluations which individual people or even entire nations make regarding their own actions. There can be no doubt that the British portrayed their actions in and around East Africa in the nineteenth century as part of a noble and heroic crusade to suppress slavery. Nowhere is this awful cant more clearly revealed than at the Berlin Conference, which began in 1884.

Until the 1870s, what is now Germany consisted of various small principalities and districts of which most people today have never even heard, such as Schleswig-Holstein, Württemberg and Westphalia. Otto von Bismarck, the Prussian statesman, managed to unify them, first into the North German Confederation and then into what was called the German Empire. This consisted largely of what we now think of as the country of Germany. It was all very well calling this rag-tag collection of statelets an empire, but when all was said and done, it amounted in truth to just another European country. France, Britain and the Netherlands all had overseas possessions in Africa, Asia and the Americas and the Germans decided that they too deserved a proper empire. The difficulty was of course that the new nation could hardly start carving out territories in North America or South Asia without coming into conflict with other and perhaps more powerful nations. One part of the world though was still available for would-be empire builders. This was Africa.

France, Italy, Britain and Germany all had designs upon one
part of Africa or another as the nineteenth century neared its end.
Rather than fight over the question, a conference was held in Berlin
in 1884 which was intended to solve the question amicably. Austria-
Hungary, Belgium, Denmark, France, Germany, Great Britain, Italy,
the Netherlands, the Ottoman Empire, Portugal, Russia, Spain,
Sweden-Norway and the United States of America took part in this
enterprise. Some nations, Britain for example, already had substantial
amounts of territory in Africa, but Germany had nothing at all. A
contemporary cartoon shows how it was thought that Germany
viewed the conference and what their interest really amounted to.
Illustration 9 depicts Bismarck, intent on dividing up Africa in order
to give himself the largest share. It was this, what has been described
as the 'scramble for Africa', which ultimately brought an end to the
slave trade in East Africa.

One of the stated aims of the Berlin Conference was to finally
rid Africa of slavery and ensure that the slave trade involving East
Africa in particular was brought to an end. This public policy may
perhaps be viewed as a fig leaf to cover what, on the face of it, look
suspiciously like naked imperial ambitions. It is beyond the scope of
this book to explore the differing aims of the powers which attended
the Berlin Conference, but within a few years of its ending, the British
had somehow acquired the East African nations of Kenya and Uganda.
Possession of those territories, together with Zanzibar, spelled the
end of the traditional Arab trade in slaves in that part of Africa. It was
hardly possible for the Arab slave traders to sail to and from the Swahili
Coast and Zanzibar when the British were actually in occupation of
those places.

Once they had firmly established themselves in that part of the
world, every effort was made by Britain in those districts of East
Africa now under their control to demonstrate to anybody hoping
to carry on trading in slaves that they were not likely to be able to do
so with impunity. When persuasion and reason failed, military force

was used. Illustration 17 shows British forces attacking one of the stockades where Arabs kept those whom they had seized.

One corner of Africa where slavery had continued in an unbroken tradition for thousands of years, from the time of the pharaohs in fact, was Egypt. By 1867 Egypt had broken free of the Ottoman Empire and its status was that of vassal state, although in reality it was an independent country. The ruler of Egypt from 1863 was Ismail Pasha, sometimes known as Ismail the Magnificent. It was the ambitions of this man for an empire of his own which triggered the events which led to the curtailment, if not the final end, of the old slave trading routes which ran from the Swahili Coast up to the eastern Mediterranean.

Curiously enough, Ismail was himself the descendant of slaves. On his father's side he was of Albanian heritage and his mother was Circassian. Ismail's father ruled Egypt and it was expected that in due course, so would he. He was sent to Europe for his education, studying in Paris. It was while travelling around Europe that Ismail realized that slavery was utterly out of keeping in a modern country and he returned to Egypt with two determinations. One was to abolish slavery, the other to build an Egyptian empire of the kind which European countries had managed to establish. Both these ambitions would entail extending Egypt's influence and power to the south, first to Sudan and then in the direction of the East African Lakes.

With Ismail's encouragement, the British and French built the Suez Canal which connected the Red Sea with the Mediterranean. This ran through Egyptian territory, between the main bulk of the country and the Sinai Peninsula, and was of crucial strategic importance for Britain. The canal meant that Britain could maintain much more rapid communications with India, which was perhaps the most valued part of the British Empire. Rather than sailing all the way around Africa, the British could now enter the Indian Ocean directly from the Mediterranean. For that reason, the peace and stability of Egypt was vital to British interests.

At the time that the Suez Canal was opened, slavery in Egypt was widespread and openly practised. The slave traders had their own guild, and the trade was divided into those which dealt in black African slaves and those which only handled white Europeans from the shores of the Black Sea. These white slaves, known as Circassians, were purchased in Istanbul and then transported from there. Some Circassians lived on the eastern shore of the Black Sea in what is now Russia, but there were also Circassian villages in Anatolia, the central plateau of present-day Turkey. In the Ottoman Empire, white European slaves had always been preferred for anything other than the most menial or arduous work. Young boys were routinely taken from the Balkans, Albania, Macedonia and so on. These were taken to Constantinople and educated. A number of viziers, roughly equivalent to Prime Ministers, were Albanian. As the Ottoman Empire declined, it became more and more difficult to raid Europe for slaves and so the hunt for white slaves turned to the north, the Caucasus, which was in the early nineteenth century a debateable and largely untamed area near the Black Sea. Thus it was that Circassians became the commonest type of white slave in the Ottoman Empire and it is why there were many also in Egypt. Black slaves were brought up via Ethiopia or the Red Sea, along the routes at which we have already looked. Since Egypt was also responsible for the administration of Sudan, which lay to the south of Egypt, these routes were largely under Egyptian control.

Different ethnicities were considered desirable for various roles and the value of the slaves varied accordingly. Circassian females were much in demand in the harems of the very well-to-do, whereas the middle-class Egyptians were compelled to make do with light-skinned Ethiopians (Lane, 1944). As has so often been the case in history, a premium was set upon whiteness. The black slaves were used either as domestic workers or labourers, although some were drafted into the army.

Slavery simply did not fit into Ismail's vision for the modern country which he visualized Egypt becoming. He caused an opera house to be built, instituted a legislative assembly, reformed education and embarked on an ambitious programme of building railways, which eventually stretched into Sudan. In 1874, he annexed part of Sudan known as Darfur and then tried to seize part of Ethiopia, only to find that the Ethiopians resisted his army and were even able to defeat Egypt in battle. Once he had asserted his control over Sudan, Ismail saw that by destroying the slave trade there, it might help to discourage it in Egypt itself, since most of the slaves were being imported from there. Rather than trust one of his own subordinates to tackle the problem, Ismail thought it wiser to engage an outsider and the obvious choice for such a project was, he thought, somebody British. The British had been trying to stamp out the slave trade in East Africa for decades and with the assistance of the ruler of Egypt, there was a good chance that a determined and forceful man might make some headway if allowed a free hand in Sudan.

The first person chosen by Ismail Pasha for the task of eradicating slavery and the slave trade in Sudan was the previously-mentioned explorer Samuel White Baker. Born in 1821, Baker led something of an unconventional life, one which led to his not being received in respectable society. During his travels in Eastern Europe he happened to attend a slave auction of white girls in the Bulgarian town of Vidin. Baker was entranced by one girl in particular, with whom he later claimed to have fallen in love at first sight. He tried to buy her, but the local pasha outbid him, whereupon Baker bribed the girl's attendants and managed to run away with her. Although they were later married, Queen Victoria herself summed up the reason that the couple could never be received. This was because she believed that they had been 'intimate' before being legally married.

After many travels in Africa, Baker found himself appointed by Ismail as both pasha and major general and given the task in 1869 of both suppressing the slave trade in Sudan and other parts of East

Africa, while at the same time expanding Egypt's nascent empire. He proved himself just the man for building an empire, for at the head of a couple of thousand Egyptian soldiers Baker succeeded in carving out what amounted to an entirely new country, which consisted of the southern part of Sudan and also the northern part of what is now Uganda. This new territory was named Equatoria. Baker was less successful at eradicating the slave trade though. As he liaised with the Egyptian officials in Sudan, he discovered just how entrenched slavery was in East Africa. The amount of bribery and corruption was staggering and despite the most strenuous efforts, no headway could be made on that front.

After Samuel White Baker had given up in despair at ever being able to make progress as regards the slave trade, Ismail chose another Englishman, one whose name will probably be familiar to everybody in Britain. This was the military hero who is generally known today as Gordon of Khartoum. This brings us to two very interesting points. The first is the great influence which slavery in Africa had upon Britain's history, something which is often forgotten. In the case of General Gordon, his appointment as the man to root out the slave trade in Sudan led to some surprising side effects, such as the abandonment of the traditional red coats which had been the mark of the British soldier for many years. The fall of Gladstone's administration was a by-product of Gordon's subsequent death and the events precipitated by Gordon's actions also came very close to robbing Britain of its most famous Prime Minister, Winston Churchill.

Born in 1833, Charles George Gordon was a very complicated character. A career soldier in the British army, he was also a devout Christian and avowed celibate. He never married, feeling himself instead called to higher things. After serving in the Crimean War, from 1855 Gordon returned to England and then went to China where he took part in the fighting against the Taiping Rebellion. He was a charismatic figure and ultimately commanded an Imperial Chinese army which he forged into a formidable fighting force. This accounts for his other nickname, which was 'Chinese' Gordon. It was after being promoted to colonel that Gordon was offered by the Egyptian government the post of governor of the newly-created province of Equatoria. With the permission of the authorities in London, he accepted and took up the post in 1873. Both he and Ismail Pasha were determined to stamp out slavery in Sudan. His predecessor as governor, Samuel White Baker, had been unable to make much headway with this, but Gordon was a military man and had command of an Egyptian army to aid him in the task.

Of course, the fact that Gordon was a serving officer in the British Army meant that his role of Governor of Sudan fitted in neatly with Britain's own imperial designs upon Africa. They may have been prepared to allow Ismail to play at empire-building, but it is very likely that, as usual, the British game was a complex one. What is indisputably true is that Gordon was very successful in his efforts to suppress the Arab slave trade in East Africa. He prosecuted the campaign with vigour, intercepting slave caravans and freeing the slaves. The traders he arrested and despatched to prison. Gordon's strength lay in the fact that he was not only quite incorruptible but also possessed of an immense and immovable conviction that he was doing God's work by putting an end to the slave trade.

There is no doubt that Gordon's work reduced the number of slaves being transported through Sudan and Equatoria, which suited both Britain and Egypt, but there were other forces at work and these erupted soon after he had a nervous breakdown through stress and returned to Britain in 1880. So essential was control of the Suez Canal to the British that it was almost inevitable that the country through which it ran should end up under their sovereignty. When the British agreed that an officer in their army be appointed governor of a large part of East Africa, it fitted naturally into this wider picture. From the late 1870s onward, nationalism began to emerge as a political force in Egypt. This was clearly dangerous for the security of the canal. It will be remembered that the Suez War which Britain fought in 1956 was associated with this very same supposed problem. As soon as the Suez Canal was completed, the British kept a very close watch upon Egypt for any signs of instability or unrest such as would hazard this vital lifeline of the British Empire.

Following a revolt in Egypt, Ismail Pasha was deposed and replaced by his eldest son, whom both the Ottomans and British viewed as being a little more pliable and easy to control than his father. Ismail was allowed to go into voluntary exile, which was unusual in those days, most deposed heads of state ending up being murdered. He went first to Italy and then, after a little time had passed, was permitted by the sultan in Constantinople to retire to a palace in the city owned by the former Egyptian ruler. Here, the erstwhile empire builder led a life of decadence and ease. He died in 1895 in a noteworthy way. Although theoretically a Muslim, Ismail was a famously heavy drinker and while giving a party at his palace accepted a wager as to whether he would be able to drain two bottles of champagne simultaneously, in one go. He was by no means sober when he undertook to accomplish this trick and after placing the necks of both bottles in his mouth he began gulping at them furiously. The result was that the liquid flooded into his lungs and he became the first man in recorded history to drown in champagne.

It is difficult to say whether the British dreaded trouble in Egypt, as it jeopardized their interests, or welcomed it, for giving them an excuse to invade the country and secure the Suez Canal permanently. In 1881, the Egyptian army gave its backing to what amounted to a coup by a nationalist leader (Karsh, 1999). By February 1882, there was a strongly-voiced desire by many among the more educated classes in Egypt for the country to seize control of its destiny and break free of both Ottoman and European influence. When these sentiments led to anti-foreigner riots in the port city of Alexandria, in the course of which fifty Europeans were killed, Britain and France decided to act. Both nations sent warships to the area and in May, the British army invaded Egypt with the avowed intention of toppling the nationalist regime and restoring the status quo.

The Anglo-Egyptian War lasted from May to August 1882 and ended with the subjugation of the country. By agreement with the Ottoman Empire, Britain established a protectorate, giving themselves responsibility for maintaining the peace and also guarding the canal. An incidental by-product of this conflict was to be the ending of all forms of slavery in Egypt. The British now controlled, if only at arm's length, not only Egypt, but also Sudan. It was unthinkable that they would tolerate the existence and continued use of the ancient routes which for thousands of years had brought slaves to the coast of the Mediterranean.

Because the fiction was maintained that Egypt was now an independent country under British protection, pressure on the nominal rulers of the country was applied very delicately. After the Anglo-Egyptian War, British officials were appointed as governors of Sudan and those who had for so long been bringing black slaves to Egypt via this country knew that this would no longer be possible. Sudan itself though was restive and an Islamist leader emerged there who had sworn to make the country an independent Muslim nation.

It should be explained that this development was in large part a response to the actions of Charles Gordon. In a textbook instance of the law of unintended consequences, the actions of an honest man who was dedicated to putting an end to slavery actually caused an increase in the very thing he sought to eradicate. The problem was that slavery in Sudan was such an integral part of life in that part of Africa that attempts to ban it were viewed as interference in a traditional way of life. It was one thing to live theoretically under British or Egyptian authority, the people of Sudan were prepared to tolerate that. But when this was combined with a real effort to prevent them from carrying on an important commercial undertaking, one in which they had been engaged for centuries, and probably millennia, without let or hindrance, then it was another matter entirely. This was the stuff of which revolutions were made.

In Sudan in 1844 was born a baby who was named Muhammad Ahmad. The boy grew up to be deeply religious and became attached to a sect of Sufis. These are Muslim mystics who believe in direct union with God via singing and dancing, among other things. They are most familiar in the West through what are sometimes called the Whirling Dervishes, who dance to attain a state of religious ecstasy. By the time he was an adult, Muhammed Ahmad had decided that he had a destiny and that it was one both spiritual and temporal. It was revealed to him by God, or so he believed, that he was the Mahdi, something roughly equivalent to the Messiah in Judaism and Christianity. The implications of this discovery for the slave trade in Sudan, which both the Egyptians and British wished to abolish, were far from promising. It was the attempted abolition of the slave trade by the British which generated such hostility towards interference in Sudan's affairs by foreigners and propelled Muhammed Ahmad to the status of national leader. This was not the only effect though upon slavery. The rise of the Mahdi had another, one which greatly increased the number of slaves in Sudan.

By the age of 26 the self-styled Mahdi had an army of Dervishes at his command and it was at this point that he chose to abandon altogether the traditional Muslim attitude to slavery. It will be recalled that according to the Hadith, the Prophet Mohammed had directed that no Muslim should be enslaved by another Muslim and that only heathens and followers of other religions might be treated in this way. The Mahdi and his Dervishes had quite another view of the matter. For them, it was a case of those who are not with us are against us. They no longer distinguished between Muslims and non-Muslims when it came to slavery, but rather between those who supported the Mahdi and those who rejected him. Christian supporters, of whom there were some, were exempt from being enslaved, but orthodox Muslims who rejected the pretensions of the young leader could be captured in battle and then sold as slaves.

The importance of this change of perspective as relating to slavery can hardly be overstated. Sudan was a Muslim nation, but there were many traditional Muslims who rejected the ideas of the Sufis and thought that they verged on the heretical. These people, if they resisted the Mahdi and were captured, were now liable to become slaves and be sold to slave traders, which was a shocking prospect. With this one alteration of the old customs, the Mahdi was undoing much of the work against slavery which had been undertaken by Baker and Gordon. To use a colloquial expression, it gave the slave trade in East Africa a shot in the arm, one which the slave traders themselves were swift to exploit. All else apart, while the country was being torn apart by revolution and war, nobody had time to spend chasing down and suppressing the slavers. Once the self-styled Mahdi had defeated the Egyptians and was more or less running the country, the stage was set for one of the most iconic moments in late Victorian imperialism.

It was bad enough that a strategic part of Africa in which the British had an interest was fast falling under the sway of a religious fanatic, but it was also plain that all the work that had been devoted to doing away with the slave trade in that part of East Africa was being undone. The British knew that they needed to take firm action, but with the defeat of an Egyptian army and loss of all its arms and artillery, the British Prime Minister, William Gladstone, came to the conclusion that abandoning Sudan entirely was the only alternative to a huge and costly war. This was until January 1884, when Gordon, who of course knew the Sudan intimately, gave an interview to the editor of the *Pall Mall Gazette*, in which he indicated that he was ready if called upon to return to Sudan and take charge of British interests in that faraway country.

Public opinion was with 'Chinese' Gordon and Gladstone reluctantly decided that it would be a popular move to send him to Africa, although with a very limited mandate. He was simply to arrange for the evacuation of British people from the country and to assess the situation there on behalf of the government. Unfortunately,

Gordon had not fully recovered from his earlier nervous breakdown and was possessed of a death-wish. He left for Sudan fully convinced that it was his destiny to die there. What Gladstone, who was himself pretty fervent when it came to religion, could not have known was that Gordon saw himself as a Christian counter to the Mahdi and that rather than planning to evacuate Khartoum, he was determined to make a heroic last stand in the city against the advancing Dervishes. In a sense, this was the glorious death which he had been seeking for the last 30 years. As early as 1855, when he was just 22 years of age, Gordon set off to the Crimean War having written to his sister that he was off to Balaklava, 'hoping, without having a hand in it, to be killed' (Donald, 2018). No sooner was he back in Sudan than he took various steps which practically assured him of a martyr's death.

When he stopped in Egypt, en route to his destination in Sudan, Gordon had several meetings with Sir Evelyn Baring, the British Consul-General of Egypt, leaving that official rather stunned by what he gleaned of the famous 'Chinese' Gordon's intentions. Despite his very clear orders from the Prime Minister, Baring contacted London to warn the government that from what he could gather, Gordon was taking his instructions directly from the prophets of the Old Testament and that would accordingly be unlikely to follow the advice of any mortal man. Baring could already see the disaster that was bound to unfold when one religious maniac clashed with another.

No sooner did he arrive in Sudan than Gordon took steps which practically ensured not only his own death, but also the fall of Khartoum to the Dervishes commanded by the Mahdi. Before arriving at the northern Sudanese town of Berber, Gordon had already written a letter in which he admitted that, 'The moment it is known that we have given up the game every man will go over to the Mahdi'. Nevertheless, when he reached Berber he summoned a meeting of all the local tribal leaders and revealed his secret instructions to evacuate Khartoum and, in effect, abandon Sudan. It was inevitable that once this became generally known the Mahdi would be the unopposed leader of the country and every man would indeed flock to his cause. This is where the new ruling on slavery was of such significance. If once the Mahdi was the undisputed ruler of Sudan, from the coast to Central Africa, then anybody who failed to support his cause would be liable to enslavement. This was a powerful incentive to at least pay lip service to the leader of the Dervishes.

Having shown London's hand in this way, Gordon proceeded to Khartoum and, in direct defiance of his orders from Gladstone, prepared to defend the city at all costs. By March 1884, Khartoum was besieged by the Mahdi's forces and Gordon had settled comfortably into his chosen role of defender of Christianity and martyr-in-waiting. The siege of Khartoum dragged on for nine months, but this was largely due to Gordon's obstinacy and refusal to obey the orders which he received from London. Although the telegraph line to Cairo had been cut, messages could still enter and leave the city, carried by runners. It was by this means that one of Gordon's last letters was despatched to his sister. He expressed the ardent hope that it was God's will for him to die there, because, 'Earth's Joys grow very dim; its glories have faded' (Donald, 2018).

In Britain, the newspapers began agitating for a rescue mission to be launched to save Khartoum and even Queen Victoria took an interest in the matter, speaking to the Prime Minister on the subject. By this time, Gladstone must have bitterly regretted being manoeuvred into sending Gordon to Sudan in the first place. By the summer, the clamour of public opinion had reached a crescendo and could no longer be ignored. Plans were laid for an expedition to relieve the siege, which was to be led by Sir Garnet Wolseley. The most infuriating aspect of the whole affair for the Prime Minister was that all Gordon needed to do was to obey orders and abandon Khartoum and return to Egypt.

The British column intended to relieve Khartoum did not arrive in Sudan until the end of January 1885, by which time the citizens of Khartoum were starving and food supplies were on the verge of running out altogether. Gordon was chain-smoking and spending his days reading the Old Testament. On the night of 25 January 1885, the besieging army launched a final assault against the city, breaking through the walls. Gordon fought to the last, by some accounts firing his revolver at the attackers while at the same time quoting scripture at them. After his death, his corpse was decapitated and the head taken to the Mahdi. The entire garrison of which he had command were slaughtered to a man. Many of the women and children were taken off into slavery (Snook, 2013).

Charles Gordon achieved his life's ambition of martyrdom. The image of a chain-smoking religious maniac firing his pistol and shouting incoherently about smiting the heathen was not really what suited those who wished to perpetuate the narrative of the British Empire. Instead, the story was sedulously circulated that Gordon had emerged at the top of a flight of stairs outside his quarters, wearing a full-dress uniform. The crowd of Dervishes had fallen silent at the sight of this imposing figure and were awestruck by his dignity and lack of fear. Then, one coward hurled a spear, and the spell was broken. A painting was commissioned of this gallant scene and it is in this way that Gordon is now remembered by most people. His death became a byword for British pluck. Illustration 13 shows Gordon as the Victorians envisaged him. He was one of the greatest heroes of the age. We are irresistibly reminded of the line from the John Wayne Western, *The Man Who Shot Liberty Valance*. At the end of the film, a journalist realizes that the story of Liberty Valance's death is just a fantasy which has grown over the years. He rips up the notes which he has made, outlining his discovery of the facts behind the myth and utters the immortal line, 'When the legend becomes fact, print the legend'.

The legend of General Gordon and the fall of Khartoum was to have a number of important and far-reaching consequences, all triggered ultimately by the desire of the British to put an end to the slave trade in East Africa. The British public took Gordon to their hearts and he came to symbolize the gallant empire builder who met his death with admirable aplomb. Of course, the Dervishes killed him, but a scapegoat was needed nearer home, somebody whom the enraged newspaper readers could blame for his death. Ironically, it was the Prime Minister, William Gladstone, upon whom the anger was focussed. Gladstone of course had not wanted to send Gordon in the first place and knew better than anybody that his death was a direct result of his refusal to obey orders, but there it was. Somebody had to be held to account and the blame was laid at Gladstone's door for being too tardy in despatching the relief column to Khartoum.

The fighting in Sudan did not end with the relief of Khartoum. Indeed, a year later skirmishes and the occasional pitched battle were still taking place, One of these was notable as a historical curiosity which has nothing at all to do with slavery, but is of interest anyway. The Battle of Ginnis, on 30 December 1885, was fought against an army of Dervishes, who despite the death of the Mahdi were still determined to drive the British and Egyptians from their land. A large force occupied the area around a British base at Ginnis, not far from Khartoum, and made life very uncomfortable for the soldiers in the fort. In the end, the decision was made to meet the enemy in open battle. It was thought that the Dervishes did not fully understand with whom they were dealing and that perhaps they believed that only Egyptians were stationed at Ginnis. For this reason, it was decided that when the British marched into position for the engagement, they would wear their traditional red coats. The idea was that once the enemy realized that they were facing British troops, they would flee in terror or, at the very least, that their morale would be badly shaken (Crawford, 2010).

Sad to relate, the appearance of what were unmistakably British troops in their famous red coats did not have the salutary effect which the commanders had hoped for. The only practical result was that the Dervishes found their enemies to be easier targets as the scarlet jackets stood out so vividly against the dusty backdrop. This was to be the last time that the red coats were seen in action. Although they were retained for ceremonial purposes and can be seen to this day guarding the king at Buckingham Palace, this style of uniform was dropped for good after the Battle of Ginnis. From then on, only khaki would be worn by British soldiers on active service.

There was to be a ghastly coda to the death of Charles Gordon after his strenuous efforts to put an end to slave trading in East Africa. This came when a British army commanded by Horatio Herbert Kitchener, whose face would later become iconic in First World War recruiting posters, crushed once and for all the Dervish forces which had caused so much trouble to British interests in Sudan. There was an element of vindictiveness about this planned attack, in that it was payback for Gordon's death and the idea was to inflict a punishment on the restless tribes of the Sudan, rather than for any real strategic purpose.

Kitchener was not a particularly brilliant soldier, but what he lacked in military acumen he made up for on this occasion by his ruthlessness and determination to show the Dervishes that they could not treat a British general as they had done without serious consequences, even if those consequences arrived over a decade later. He had known Gordon, which gave Kitchener a personal reason for causing as much harm to the Sudanese warriors as he could.

After the fall of Khartoum and the death of the Mahdi, the Dervishes had abandoned the city and establish a new capital at Omdurman and it was here that the climax of Kitchener's campaign took place. Incredibly, even with all the resources of the world's most powerful industrial nation, it still took Kitchener two and a half years to conquer Sudan. This was not because he faced serious opposition and prolonged bouts of fighting, but rather because he and his forces moved south with glacial slowness. Kitchener was in no hurry at all and was more concerned with making a thorough job of things than he was in any fancy manoeuvres or taking any unnecessary risks. With his army rode a young officer attached to the 21st Lancers who was also an official war correspondent for *The Morning Post*. This was the 23-year-old Winston Churchill.

The ultimate aim of what was essentially a punitive expedition was the Dervish capital of Omdurman and despite the overwhelming firepower possessed by the British forces, the Battle of Omdurman almost turned into a fiasco. That it did not, but rather cemented Kitchener's reputation as the finest soldier of his generation and the perfect figure for recruiting posters 16 years later, was largely a matter of chance.

When Kitchener finally reached the outskirts of Omdurman in 1898, years after leaving Britain, his first act was to desecrate the tomb of the Mahdi. He dynamited the stone structure and then had the bones thrown in a nearby river. The skull he kept for himself and had turned into an inkwell. Queen Victoria was disgusted when she heard about this action and ordered the commander of the expedition to replace the skull in the remains of the tomb (Regan, 1993). After having demonstrated his contempt for the man responsible for General Gordon's death, Kitchener prepared for the climactic battle of his campaign. He had at his disposal 25,000 soldiers, 44 field guns and 10 gunboats. These boats, which were bristling with artillery, had been sailed part of the way up the Nile and then dismantled and carried overland. They were to prove their worth in the course of the coming battle. Ranged against this formidable military force was a huge army, but one in which more men were equipped with spears and swords than had modern repeating rifles.

The first phase of the Battle of Omdurman went as smoothly as anybody could hope for. Just after dawn on 2 September 1898, scouts reported that a large force of Dervishes were heading for the British camp. Something in the region of 50,000 warriors were bearing down on Kitchener's position, but this was just as he wished. They might have been outnumbered two to one, but the Sudanese had no artillery or gunboats. At 6:50 AM, the British artillery opened fire, as did the 12-pounder guns and machine guns on the boats anchored nearby. Great swathes of the attacking force were cut down and then Kitchener ordered his men to stand shoulder to shoulder and fire at will into the screaming tribesman who were now half a mile or so away. Not one of the attackers got within a quarter of a mile of the British lines. It was a massacre. The only remark made by Kitchener about the slaughter which he and his forces had inflicted on lightly-armed opponents was to say to an aide, 'What a dreadful waste of ammunition!'

That Kitchener was no great strategist may be seen from his next move. He assumed that after this first charge had been repelled that the battle was now ended and all that remained was to finish the lesson which he had taught the followers of the late Mahdi by despatching his cavalry to harry them as they retreated. What he did not know was that this first attack had involved only a quarter of the army which was gathered in and about Omdurman, and that one body of men almost 40,000 strong was still in the area, together with smaller groups, although even these other groups numbered in the thousands. Despite being unaware of the disposition of any other enemy forces near at hand, Kitchener order a cavalry unit, the 21st Lancers, to pursue what he thought were the fleeing remnants of the Dervish forces. His orders to Colonel Martin, the commander of the 21st, indicated clearly that for Kitchener, the fighting was essentially over. Writing of the men fleeing from the massacre which he had inflicted, Kitchener ordered the cavalry to, 'Annoy them as far as possible on their flank and head them off if possible from Omdurman' (Regan, 1993).

The 21st Lancers were the only unit in the campaign without any battle honours and their commander was determined to rectify this humiliating state of affairs. Just following the retreating foot solders of the Dervish army would be unlikely to stand out as a conspicuous act of valour by the troops whom he led and so Martin decided that a full-scale charge by his cavalry would be an impressive affair. It all looked so easy and straightforward. A straggling line of Dervishes was hurrying away across the sand and so the colonel ordered the bugler to sound a charge and he and his 400 troopers galloped after the retreating enemy. It was only when the riders reached a crest in the sand dunes that they realized that they had been led into a trap. More than 2,000 warriors lay waiting in a wadi, a dried-up watercourse. From being an exciting and safe piece of military pageantry, the charge of the 21st Lancers had suddenly and unexpectedly turned into a life or death struggle for survival.

Among the officers and men who had galloped headlong into the ambush was Winston Churchill.. Like all the other British cavalry, he found himself outnumbered five to one and fighting for his life (Ziegler, 1990). Fortunately, the future Prime Minister was able to escape unscathed, but the same cannot be said for many others who took part in that fatal and ill-judged action. No fewer than five officers, 65 troopers and 119 horses were killed or injured during this unnecessary engagement. It was the greatest loss of life in the Battle of Omdurman.

The invasion of Sudan, which climaxed in the Battle of Omdurman, left nobody in any doubt that East Africa fell within the British sphere of influence. The ironic thing is that although this now gave Britain control over the routes traditionally used to bring slaves north to Egypt and then to the rest of the Ottoman Empire, it was not this physical occupation of territory which ultimately brought to an end the practice of owning slaves in Egypt, which also cut off the supply to other Ottoman provinces. It was social pressure and economic expedience, rather than military conquest, which effected this change.

Although Ismail Pasha had been overthrown and driven into exile, his ideas of modernization and desire for Egypt to become an up-to-date nation had taken root. Educated Egyptians were well aware that slavery was an anachronism as the nineteenth century drew on. The United States had abandoned the practice after the end of the American Civil War and only in Africa was slavery really flourishing; there and in the decadent Ottoman Empire. Egypt hoped though to align itself more with Europe and there, slavery was regarded with horror and disgust. Then too, there was the point made by Adam Smith a century earlier, that reliance upon slaves works to stifle innovation and industrialization. Much of the most arduous work in

Egypt, such as turning waterwheels to draw up water from the Nile, was undertaken by gangs of black slaves, some of whom may be seen in Illustration 20.

Ultimately, slavery in Egypt ended, and the routes along which slaves were brought into the country withered away, not because of any military action on the part of the British Empire, but for the same reasons that the British themselves had abandoned slavery earlier in the century. It was a desire for progress and a rejection of outdated ways of doing things which sound the death-knell for slavery in that particular corner of Africa.

Chapter 10

Slavery in Twentieth-Century Africa

It has always been easier to prevent the maritime trade in slaves than it has been to end the practice of slavery itself. This is especially so in Africa, many parts of which were, and indeed still are, either wholly inaccessible to outsiders or very difficult to reach. Even in countries which were colonial possessions, the most that the Europeans could hope to do was ensure that slavery did not take place in cities and large towns and the land surrounding them for some miles. What went on in remote rural districts was impossible to police. A perfect instance of this may be seen in the British administration of the territory of Sierra Leone.

Sierra Leone was a colony set up by Britain in the late eighteenth century to provide a place where freed slaves and what were known as the 'black poor' of London could live free and profitable lives. Britain chose a part of West Africa and then delineated what they thought the proper boundaries of the new colony should be, without reference to the Africans who already lived there. This not unnaturally caused friction between the former slaves and indigent black people from London who arrived there from 1787 onward and those who were already living in the new country. The colony struggled to survive in its early years in the face of hostility from the people who had been living there long before the British landed and saw their land being usurped. Somehow though, Sierra Leone kept going and remained a British possession until the 1960s.

One surprising feature of Sierra Leone is that although it had belonged to the British since 1787, slavery was only abolished there in 1928, ten years after the end of the First World War. This may surprise some people who were under the impression that slavery was abolished throughout the whole of the British Empire in 1839. This is of course perfectly true, but the British Empire was never a homogenous entity and consisted of all kinds of different bits with varying legal positions. Freetown, the capital of Sierra Leone, was used as a base by the British for the administration of all their territories in West Africa, including the Gold Coast, which is today known as Ghana. Because Freetown was a colony, the usual laws of the British Empire applied to it. However, the land surrounding the city for hundreds of miles, although technically British territory, had never been formally acquired by Britain. These areas were annexed in 1896 and declared to be the Sierra Leone Protectorate. This meant that it was a separate legal entity from Freetown itself and the laws relating to slavery did not apply outside the city (Harris, 2012). Since slavery was an old African custom in most parts of the continent and nobody seemed minded to interfere with what was going on outside Freetown, it continued to flourish in Sierra Leone, even after annexation.

The chief ethnic group in the protectorate who practised slavery were called the Mende and although even in the twentieth century they had no intention of giving it up, they were aware that the British administrators rather disapproved of it. For this reason they did their best to persuade the colonial authorities, against all the evidence, that what they saw when they visited Mende villages was not actually slavery at all, but something far more benign (Miers and Kopytoff, 1977). This was not all that hard to do, because the finer points of the language used were sometimes misleading, even when a British official actually understood the language fluently. For instance the Mende word for slave was *nduwe* but the Mende assured the British that this did not have the same connotations which were often associated with the word 'slave' in English. It was claimed that a relationship more like that of family members existed between the Mende and their slaves. The slaves, after all, addressed their masters as *keke*, which means 'father'. There was no real equivalence though. Even old men who were slaves were addressed as 'boy'. Readers may be reminded of the practice in the southern states of America, which was still extant in living memory, of calling black men of any age 'boy'. This custom was of course observed in the American Deep South when slavery was still in existence. Some British officials were not at all deceived by all this. In 1924 a District Commissioner wrote an interesting book called *Outline of Native Law in Sierra Leone*. He was quite clear that what he witnessed was chattel slavery;

> The slave is not a person; he cannot make a contract; he can have little interest in his work . . . At any time the master may consider his slave guilty of misbehaviour or disobedience and at once depress him to his theoretical condition of duties without rights. The slave becomes simply property. (Fenton, 1924)

'The slave becomes simply property.' This sentence alone tells us that the Mende customs, whatever they might pretend to the contrary, were none other than chattel slavery.

At least in Sierra Leone, those keeping slaves knew that they were under observation by the British and even if this was not sufficient to prevent the practice entirely, at the very least it had the effect of mitigating some of its harsher aspects. The Mende knew that while the keeping of domestic servants whose status was dubious might be permitted, they would certainly be called to account if they were to start murdering or mutilating such individuals. There might even be serious repercussions if a slave were to go missing and it was discovered that he had been sold. After slavery was officially forbidden in the protectorate, this was all the more the case and owners went to considerable lengths to ensure that nothing happened to their slaves which would invite awkward questions from the colonial authorities. In those parts of Africa where no European authority was to be feared, however, matters were a good deal worse.

Ethiopia has never been colonized and has moreover a recorded history dating back thousands of years. This means that, unlike the pre-literate societies which existed in most of sub-Saharan Africa, we have a fairly good idea what has gone on in the country since the time of Christ. One of the things which has gone on is of course the use of, and trade in, slaves.

Ethiopia was ideally positioned from a geographical point of view to be a slave-trading nation. On the one hand, it is perfectly situated as a land route from sub-Saharan Africa to Sudan and Egypt. There is too the fact that it is only separated from the Arabian Peninsula by a narrow strait of the Red Sea. It is not hard to see how those wishing to bring slaves from Africa to the Arab world should find Ethiopia a convenient crossroads. Throughout the nineteenth century, the slave trade continued in Ethiopia as it had done since time immemorial and the dawning of the twentieth century made no appreciable difference. Slaves were still being taken from outlying parts of the country and then transported by sea to Arabia or India. Others were taken by land to Egypt. Some of the slaves were young women, bound for the harems of the Ottoman Empire.

It was not until Haile Selassie ascended the throne as emperor in 1930 that any real effort was made to curb the slave trade. Before becoming emperor, he had toured Europe and the Middle East, visiting London, Paris, Amsterdam, Geneva, Stockholm, Athens and Jerusalem. During his time in Europe, the soon-to-be ruler of Ethiopia gauged the mood of the civilized world quite correctly to be set dead against slavery. The newly formed League of Nations, a predecessor of the United Nations, was campaigning to end slavery of all kinds and when he returned to his own country and assumed the throne, Haile Selassie was determined to be a reformer and to bring his nation into the twentieth century. Like the British colonial authorities in other parts of Africa though, he found it easier to pass laws and make firm pronouncements than to ensure that things really changed. Just like the British, he could insist that in his capital city there should be no signs of slavery or the slave trade, but changing the habits which had existed for many lifetimes in the backwaters of the country was another matter entirely.

We touched earlier in this book on the matter of ethnicity in Ethiopia. That the rulers of the country have for thousands of years been the descendants of people who colonized the country is wholly unknown to the average person, who assumes that Ethiopia is a proud African nation which has always been independent and was never a European colonial possession, other than for a few brief years following the Italian invasion in 1935. This is not really the case at all. A glance at any photograph of Haile Selassie will be enough to tell anybody that he was not at all a typical sub-Saharan African and that there was a distinctly Levantine look to his appearance. This is because the elite and the ruling class in Ethiopia were at that time in a similar position to the British in Nigeria and Sierra Leone.

The high-status language of Ethiopia is of course Amharic, which has a written form dating back 3,000 years. The earliest inscriptions in Ethiopia in the Ge'ez script, which evolved into modern written Amharic, date to roughly 900 BC. They are in a form of script identical to that being used in the southern part of the Arabian Peninsula at that time. The modern languages of Amharic, together with the Tigrinya spoken in Eritrea, are both Semitic, which is to say that they are related to Hebrew and Arabic (Dalby, 1998). Many of the words in all these languages are identical, which clearly shows their common origin. In Ethiopia a lot more people speak Oromo than do Amharic, but Oromo is a purely African language and is regarded by Amharic speakers as being of lower status for that reason. This linguistic and ethnic divide is germane to the discussion of slavery in twentieth-century Ethiopia, because the slave traders and owners of slaves were Amharic speakers of Semitic ancestry, in contrast to the slaves, who were usually black African. There was no inclination on the part of the slave traders to give up such a profitable business just because the young new emperor had been gadding about in foreign countries picking up a lot of new ideas and trying to revolutionize an ancient way of life. They had history on their side, because Haile Selassie was not the first emperor of Ethiopia to try and abolish slavery. In 1854 Emperor Tewodros II attempted to put an end to slavery and failed. Thirty years later Emperor Yohannes IV also made an effort to suppress the slave trade, but this too proved ineffective (Pankhurst, 1968).

The number of slaves in Ethiopia in 1932, a couple of years after Haile Selassie came to power, was estimated at a fifth of the total population of the country (Noel-Buxton, 1932). If so, this would mean that more than three million slaves were living in Ethiopia in the early years of Haile Selassie's reign. Slavery was so deeply embedded within the culture of the country that abolishing it was never likely to prove a simple and straightforward task, certainly not one which could be accomplished by the emperor's signature on a proclamation.

Ethiopia was a Christian country and had been since the time of the Axumite empire. The church itself, the Ethiopian Orthodox Church, was very firmly in favour of slavery. It may seem almost beyond belief, but the church justified the practice by appealing to the Curse of Ham at which we looked in an earlier chapter. The Amharic-speaking inhabitants of the country saw themselves as an elite and did not think in terms of being black. The black people spoke African languages and their skins were darker. It was therefore, at least according to many clerics of the Ethiopian Orthodox Church, perfectly in accordance with scripture to own and trade in black slaves (Hellie, 1993). The church in Ethiopia also endorsed an old and time-honoured custom, in that they believed that it was acceptable to enslave prisoners of war. In Ethiopia, this principle was enshrined in the *Fetha Nagast* code. This was a set of legal precepts compiled by a Coptic Christian writing in Egypt in the thirteenth century. From the fifteenth century, it served in Ethiopia as a constitution; a role which it fulfilled until 1932 (Moore-Harell, 1999).

Ethiopia was known for the part of the twentieth century at which we are now looking as Abyssinia, but it might prove easier to use one name, rather than to resort to the use of brackets and explanatory notes. This might give a slight air of anachronism at times. Although Ethiopia had succeeded in remaining as a wholly independent Africa state at a time when the rest of the continent was being divided up between European nations in the process known sometimes as the 'Scramble for Africa', this independence had only been maintained by military action. Italy had made a determined attempt to seize the country in 1895. This had been a failure and led to the defeat of the Italian army and their Eritrean allies at the Battle of Adwa in 1896 (Milkias and Metaferia, 2005). When Benito Mussolini came to power in Italy as a dictator in the 1920s, he promised to make his country great again and invoked the memory of the Roman Empire. The attack on Ethiopia was a part of this strategy. Just as the Germans had desired colonies in Africa in the late nineteenth century for no other reason than the prestige which they would lend the newly-unified country, so too did Mussolini believe that expanding Italy's influence into Africa would be an easy way of showing that the country was operating on equal terms with other European nations such as Britain and France.

Italy of course had a number of problems in the 1920s and 1930s. There was a worldwide recession which we know today as the Great Depression, and this affected some countries more than others. One of the most popular ways known in politics to encourage a nation to stop worrying about domestic affairs such as unemployment, the price of food and standard of living is to distract attention from these problems by a short and successful foreign war. The classic instance of this is the actions of the British Prime Minister Margaret Thatcher in the spring of 1982. At the beginning of 1982, after almost three years in power. Margaret Thatcher's popularity with the British public had reached a very low point indeed. Unemployment was at record levels, reminiscent of the Great Depression of the 1930s, and the standard of living for most people was definitely not rising. The following year, she won a truly astonishing landslide victory in a General Election; the greatest victory of an incumbent Prime Minister in living memory. How had she achieved this miraculous turnabout in her political fortunes? It was very simple. When Argentina invaded an insignificant British territory in the South Atlantic, Thatcher launched a spectacularly successful military operation to retake the tiny islands which had been occupied by enemy troops. This victory was just what people needed to take their minds off unemployment, terrorism and various other undesirable features of life in their country. A surge of patriotism swept the country and Thatcher rode this wave back into Downing Street a year later.

Mussolini's real aim in invading Ethiopia was to demonstrate to the Italian people that they were to have an empire again, one which would perhaps rival that of Rome. This would serve in a most spectacular way to distract attention from any domestic problems which might otherwise engage their attention. Despite the popular belief that Mussolini kept the trains running on time, ordinary people in Italy still faced many difficulties after he came to power. Even the idea of the trains running on time is something of a myth (Seldes, 1935). The main lines used by tourists might have improved, but the trains used by the Italians themselves on smaller lines were as inefficient as always.

The small territory of Eritrea and part of Somalia were already Italian possessions and since these neatly sandwiched Ethiopia, it was plain that an attack on two fronts would be possible. There was a problem though and that was that however well an invasion of Ethiopia might play in his own country, it was the sort of action which was apt to raise eyebrows in the rest of the world. In particular, the League of Nations, the forerunner of the present United Nations, would need to be shown that Mussolini's actions in conquering an African country were something more than mere empire-building. A ready-made excuse presented itself. The League of Nations was very concerned in the years leading up to the start of the Second World War with the question of slavery of all kinds and it was this concern which Mussolini exploited to great effect.

In 1926 the League of Nations estimated that there were between two and five million slaves in the world. As with similar claims in modern times by the United Nations, many of these people were not what most of us would really describe as slaves. The number included forced marriages, child apprentices and conscripted labour. Even so, it was undeniably the case that genuine and unmistakable slavery was still being practised in Africa and that Ethiopia was, as it had been since time out of mind, a conduit for slaves being taken from to the Middle East from sub-Saharan Africa. In 1934 Colonel Bernard Reilly held the post of Commissioner in the Yemen, at a time when the British had a colonial presence there. Because it is only separated from the African mainland by a few miles at the Bab el Mandeb, Yemen has always been a most convenient staging post for those transporting African slaves to other parts of the Arabian Peninsula. Colonel Reilly wrote a formal letter to the Imam, who was officially the ruler of the country, seeking an assurance that the slave trade from Ethiopia would be brought to an end. It read as follows:

> I have the honour to refer to my conversations with your Majesty's plenipotentiary relating to the present common desire of all enlightened nations to co-operate in the suppression of the slave trade, and to enquire whether your Majesty will enable me to convey to his Britannic Majesty's Government your Majesty's assurance that you will, by every possible means, assist them in their endeavours to prevent the African slave trade by sea. (Reilly, 1960)

It is a little disconcerting to read, as late as the 1930s, about efforts to try and prevent 'the African slave trade by sea'. The Imam replied in the most flowery language, recognizing quite correctly that the British were, in effect, saying 'Sort it out, or else!' He wrote:

> In the Name of God, the Merciful and Compassionate! After tendering our sincere respects, in reply to your esteemed

> note . . . we agree to the prohibition of the African slave
> traffic . . . (Reilly, 1960)

Just as with the Emperor of Ethiopia's efforts, many assurances were
sought and given, but things carried on much as before, except that
the slave traders behaved with a good deal more discretion.

As early as December 1934 there had been skirmishes between
Ethiopian troops and Italian soldiers on the border of the Italian part
of Somalia (Gilbert, 1998). Matters rumbled on throughout 1935,
with other incidents, until at dawn on 3 October an army commanded
by General Emilio de Bono crossed the border from Italian-controlled
Eritrea and moved south into Ethiopia. Four days later, as the Italian
army swept through Ethiopia, the League of Nations declared the
invasion to be a war of aggression and began the cumbersome and time-
consuming process of instituting sanctions against Mussolini's regime.
Italy though made a good deal of political capital of the indisputable
fact that the country they were now advancing through contained
hundreds of thousands, perhaps millions, of slaves. It was claimed
that the invasion was in some way a humanitarian enterprise whose
chief aim was to liberate slaves. As part of this propaganda campaign,
a proclamation was issued by General de Bono on 14 October 1935
which announced the abolition of slavery in the areas under Italian
control. The results of this were not perhaps as impressive as could
have been desired. The general wrote:

> I am obliged to say that the proclamation did not have much
> effect on the owners of slaves and perhaps still less on the
> liberated slaves themselves. Many of the latter, the instant they
> were set free, presented themselves to the Italian authorities,
> asking 'And now who gives me food? (Barker, 1971)

Another proclamation on the abolition of slavery by the Italians in April
1936 had a similar effect to the first. Notwithstanding the fact that
Italy claimed to have freed 420,000 slaves by these measures, business

continued pretty much as it had done for the last few thousand years. If the Ethiopians were not minded to obey their own emperor in this matter, it is hardly likely that they would take more notice of a foreign army of occupation. Haile Selassie had sought refuge abroad following the fall of Addis Ababa, the capital of Ethiopia. When the Italians were forced to surrender the country during the Second World War, he returned and at once promulgated a new written constitution, designed to replace the ancient *Fetha Nagast*. This included a specific passage abolishing slavery and the trade in slaves in Ethiopia.

The difficulty with passing laws to forbid any mercantile activity involving a commodity which many people want, and this is as true of slaves as it is of drugs or firearms, is that there will always be found people who are prepared to disregard the law if the potential profits are high enough. In the case of slaves being taken to Arabia, the demand was high and so were the profits. In fact, the slavers were not even breaking the law in some of the nations in the Middle East. Slavery remained legal in Kuwait until 1947 and Qatar until 1952. In the Sultanate of Muscat and Oman, the traditional ruler of Zanzibar and the Swahili Coast, slavery was not made illegal until 1970. That it was flourishing in parts of Arabia after the Second World War is freely acknowledged. Professor Gabriel Baer, a German-born orientalist, wrote in the early 1960s that 'Slaves are still to be found in the Aden Protectorate, Trucial Oman, Yemen and, most of all, in Saudi Arabia'.

It was in the more remote and less accessible parts of Africa that slavery flourished most in the twentieth century. This was particularly so in debatable lands close to the border between one country and another. In such locations both countries concerned could avoid the trouble of launching campaigns to eradicate the practice by affecting to believe that the problem was really the proper responsibility of their neighbour. So it was that in a district in Nigeria which was very close to the border with Cameroon, some of the older and less palatable customs associated with slavery were able to continue into modern times.

In the far north of the West African country of Cameroon lies a range of mountains known as the Mandara. These mountains effectively delineate the border between Cameroon and Nigeria. There is little of interest in this mountainous area; no minerals, agricultural land or anything else much. The governments of both Nigeria and Cameroon have historically been content to leave those living in this sparsely inhabited and remote area to their own devices. This was the custom in colonial times and it has persisted to this day. The people who live mostly on the Nigerian side of the border, in the lowlands beneath the Mandara mountains, are called the Margi. This group of tribes have occupied the area, according to oral tradition, for something in excess of 300 years. Although nominally citizens of Nigeria or Cameroon, neither nation really troubles the Margi, which goes some way towards explaining why, until at least the 1960s, slavery persisted.

The society of the Margi had a special designation for certain of those living among them, for which the word '*mafa*' was used (Miers and Kopytoff, 1977). In 1959 and 1960 James Vaughan of Indiana University conducted field research among the Margi and discovered that none of the people to whom he spoke even knew that the institution of slavery was illegal. As he wrote some years later in 1977,

> Margiland is remote, and the forces of change had been little felt in 1959 and 1960, when I collected these data, and the institution was then alive. In fact I was not aware that any local person knew it was illegal until many months had passed and the events noted below took place. (Miers and Kopytoff, 1977)

Vaughan went on to say that nobody was at all secretive about the *mafa* among them and that he met and spoke to such slaves. It was simply that slavery had been a tradition there for many centuries and nobody from the governments of either Nigeria or Cameroon seemed to have got round to telling everybody that slavery was no longer acceptable. They knew, by contrast, that witchcraft was frowned upon by the authorities and took care to hide any signs of it if outsiders were visiting, but nobody appeared to be at all worried about slavery.

There were two ways that a person in Margiland could end up as a slave. The first was something at which we have looked in some detail, which is to say being captured in warfare or as a result of raids by neighbouring peoples. The second was being made into a slave as punishment. Both of these two processes had fallen into disuse at the time that James Vaughan carried out his research and there were as a result fewer slaves than had once been the case. Those whom Vaughan encountered had either been acquired by trade or born into slavery. Just as in the Caribbean, the child of a slave was also considered to be a slave.

One thing which did become apparent was that some of the crueller and more barbarous customs which were seen in the ancient world had lingered on in this part of Africa until living memory at the time that Vaughan was visiting the area, some 60 years ago. For example, we have looked at the custom, which was of course not restricted to Africa, of killing slaves on the death a ruler, so that they could serve him in the afterlife. It is worth quoting what Vaughan has to say about this.

> When a king died, one or more *mafa* were killed and buried with him. This happened as recently as 1906. The eldest son of the king who died then not only tends a shrine to his father but a *mafa* shrine as well. The wife who cooked for a king was also put to death. (Miers and Kopytoff, 1977)

It is extraordinary to think that a little over a century ago, the old custom of killing slaves in this way and burying them with their master was still going strong in Africa. We must reflect at this point on something which was discussed earlier. There is a widespread modern tendency to attribute all the evils of slavery and the slave trade, as it affected Africa, to the machination of white imperialists. Reading material written in the last few years certainly leads young people in particular to believe that before the coming of the white man, Africa was some kind of tropical paradise where everybody lived happily, at peace with one another and in tune with nature. According to this perspective, slavery was something imposed upon Africa from outside and this was done by Europeans.

Reading what James Vaughan discovered when he lived among the Margi makes it as plain as a pikestaff that in areas where there was little or no outside influence, slavery was practised as a matter of routine. The effect of colonial influence, especially in those parts of Africa in which Britain had an interest, was to reduce slavery and strongly discourage the slave trade by means of armed force. Vaughan was in Nigeria the year that it became an independent country, after almost 50 years of British rule. During that time, despite British opposition, slavery simply continued as it had done for centuries or millennia. The keeping of *mafa* by the Margi was not something which had begun with British rule and nor was it an imitation of a white European custom. On the contrary, it was a purely African tradition; the sort of thing which happened across the whole of the continent.

Chapter 11

Slavery in Modern Africa

It is often claimed that there are now more slaves in the world than at any other time in human history. Estimated numbers exceed 46 million people enslaved in various ways (*Guardian*, 2006). There is a slight problem with this idea, widely believed though it may be. This is that although there are indeed still slaves in the world, very few of them fall into the same category as the chattel slaves at whom we have mainly been looking in this book. They are rather victims of what is described as 'modern slavery'. This does not mean, as one might be forgiven for supposing, chattel slaves in the modern world. It means instead people in a variety of categories which entail working under compulsion or in unpleasant and degrading circumstances, which is a different matter entirely. In short, the problem is one of semantics. Before looking at the definition of modern slavery, one or two examples might enable readers to judge for themselves whether or not what this term encompasses is the same as, or even comparable with, the systems at which we have so far been looking.

Imagine for a moment a boy begging on a street corner in London. He is from an Eastern European country. At the end of the day, a man collects him, takes a cut of the money which he has collected and then delivers him to the relatives with whom he is living. This is without doubt an undesirable and exploitative situation, but are we really justified in using the same world for this state of affairs as that which we applied to the women seized in Somalia in the nineteenth century and sold to a harem of the Ottoman Empire? What of a young Vietnamese woman smuggled into Britain and provided with rough accommodation in a house divided up like a dormitory. She is sent to work in a nail-bar and ends up working long hours, being paid less than the minimum wage. This too is described as 'modern slavery' but cannot in all honesty be compared with the slaves captured in Africa and transported to the plantations of the Caribbean.

Modern slavery, which is without doubt a most awful business, includes forced marriages, prostitution, begging, prison labour, conscription, forced labour and child labour. Clearly, these are none of them pleasant things, but most of us would draw a distinction between a young woman pressured by her family into an arranged marriage with an older man and the fate of a slave on a plantation in Georgia before the American Civil War. For this reason, we shall limit our examination of slavery in the present day to the kind of thing which we have been examining, which is to say slavery by capture in war, purchase or descent. Two of these types of slavery are still flourishing in Africa, although the numbers involved certainly do not run into the tens of millions.

Slavery by descent was of course the rule in all the cultures at which we have so far looked. A baby born to a slave inherits automatically his or her mother's status. The position is precisely similar to that of domestic animals. If I own a horse and the animal gives birth to a foal, then as a matter of course, the foal is also my possession. Although this is a distasteful subject to consider, slavery by descent is still going strong in some African countries, most notably Mauritania.

Mauretania was at one time a French colonial possession and in 1905, slavery was outlawed there. As we have seen though, it was not easy for colonial administrations actually to abolish slavery in Africa. It was simple enough to make an announcement and even to threaten terrible penalties for those who kept slaves or engaged in the trading of them, but enforcing such edicts was another matter entirely. This was particularly so in a large territory like Mauretania, which covers some 800,000 square miles; roughly five times the area of Great Britain. The slavery which lingers on to this day in Mauritania is a legacy of the North African slave trade, in which Arabs and Berbers carried black African slaves from their homes and took them to the Barbary States which fringed the Mediterranean. It is for this reason still based today on ethnic and religious grounds.

There are two main ethnic groups in Mauretania; namely the Berbers and those of mixed Berber and Arab descent who constitute about 30 per cent of the population, and the indigenous black Africans. The Berbers refer to themselves as white and tend to regard themselves as an elite. Historically, they owned slaves belonging to the Haritine ethnic group, who today make up about 40 per cent of the people in the country. It is members of this group who are still held as slaves by many Berber families.

Mauretania was the last country in the world to outlaw slavery, which was done by presidential decree in 1981. This move was welcomed, but there was a catch. Although slavery had definitely been forbidden, no laws relating to criminal prosecution were passed. This meant that those holding slaves, as they had done for centuries, faced no legal sanctions. So it was that for the next quarter of a century after its supposed abolition, slavery continued in Mauretania much as it had for the last thousand years or so. Just to be clear, this was chattel slavery: the Haritine slaves were born into slavery and were the possessions of their owners. Women could be raped by the men who owned them and their babies then became slaves in turn. It is impossible to say how many slaves there were in the country as the twenty-first century dawned, because it was in nobody's particular interest to find out. A rough estimate is that two per cent of the population of Mauretania, perhaps 90,000 people, are chattel slaves. Many more are held in bondage of one kind or another.

In Mauretania we are able to see the remnants of the old Arab and Berber slave trade, dating back to the time when caravans of black Africans were marched north across the desert to the territories on the Mediterranean coast. In another part of Africa though, there is an even older type of slavery, one where one group of black Africans have enslaved another. In Chapter 3 we looked at the way in which the

Bantus left their homeland in West Africa and spread out, colonizing the entire continent. As they did so, between four and a half and two thousand years ago, they took over the rain forest in which dwelt the Pygmies.

The Bantu were both workers in iron and also agriculturalists. This meant that as they occupied an area, they chopped down trees, ploughed the land and planted crops. Because they had no means of fertilizing fields once a crop had been grown and so extracted the nutrients from the soil, their practice was simply to move on to a new area and hack down more forest to create another stretch of arable land. The Pygmies, by contrast, were hunter-gatherers. They roamed a large part of the rain forest, catching what animals they were able and also collecting roots and berries. The destruction of their habitat was catastrophic for them. The result of this clash of cultures was grimly inevitable. The Pygmies were deprived of their land and many were enslaved, a situation which exists to this day.

In the Republic of the Congo, which was once the heartland of the Pygmies' territory, Bantu now make up between 90 and 98 per cent of the population. The few remaining Pygmies are, according to one Congolese source, 'treated like pets'. This is simply another way of indicating that the Pygmies are subject to chattel slavery; that they are regarded as being owned by another person. This is 'slavery by descent', just like that practised in Mauretania. Bantu families own families of Pygmies who have served their own families for generations. They are expected to work for their owners but are not paid wages. Instead, they are provided with cigarettes or second-hand clothing. The Bantu describe this arrangement as a 'time-honoured tradition' and there is no reason to suppose that they are cruel to their Pygmies, nor do they mistreat them at all. They are even regarded with some affection, but this does not alter the essential nature of the relationship between the two parties. Slavery may exist even without any ill-treatment, even if the slaves are housed well and have enough to eat. During a war crimes trial in Nuremberg after the end of the

Second World War, a number of Nazis who had been responsible for supplying slave labour to industry were charged with crimes against humanity. Part of the defence was that the slaves had rations which were the same as those of their guards. Giving judgement in this case in November 1947, the tribunal ruled as follows:

> Slavery may exist even without torture. Slaves may be well fed and well clothed and comfortably housed, but they are still slaves if without lawful process they are deprived of their freedom by forceful restraint. We might eliminate all proof of ill treatment, overlook the starvation and beatings and other barbarous acts, but the admitted fact of slavery – compulsory uncompensated labour – would still remain. There is no such thing as benevolent slavery. Involuntary servitude, even tempered by humane treatment, is still slavery. (Roland, 2012)

The above judgement sums up the accepted view on slavery. Whatever affection may exist between master and slave, and there is reason to suppose that this state of affairs has not been uncommon throughout history, there really is no such thing as 'benevolent slavery'. Which means that even without the use of chains and beating, the condition of the Pygmies in the Congo and the Haritine in Mauretania amounts without any doubt at all to slavery.

Nor are these two countries the only ones in Africa where slavery is still to be found. We have seen that there is a very longstanding tradition in North Africa of the trade in black African slaves, one which dates back thousands of years. Regrettably, this has made a return in recent years, since the overthrow of the Libyan dictator Muammar Ghaddafi.

The so-called 'Arab Spring' saw the fall of governments in Tunisia and Egypt. It resulted too in the overthrow of Colonel Ghaddafi, for over 40 years the undisputed ruler of Libya. The nation then descended into chaos from which it has not, at the time of writing in the autumn of 2021, wholly recovered. In the disorder of the civil war which followed Ghaddafi's overthrow and murder, Libya became the favoured staging post for those from sub-Saharan Africa seeking to reach Europe. This was a profitable business for the warlords and people-smugglers who were able to exploit the desperation of migrants who had crossed the Sahara Desert. Many were indeed transported across the Mediterranean in small boats, but others, those without sufficient money to pay the extortionate fares being charged, found themselves penniless and alone in a foreign country where they did not speak the language. Their helplessness was exploited by unscrupulous Libyans and some found themselves being auctioned off in slave markets and sold to farmers as labourers (BBC, 2017).

When film emerged of young men from Niger being sold off to the highest bidder as farm workers, the Chair of the African Union, President Alpha Conde of Guinea, expressed his outrage and demanded that the world took action to halt such outrageous spectacles. The young men had often made their way through the desert, only to find that the prices being charged for a passage to Europe were far beyond their means. Having taken charge of them, some of the people-smugglers then tried to extort money from their families by sending messages back to their home countries. If this failed, then they would auction the hapless individuals off for what they could get; usually no more than £300 or so. The migrants themselves were hungry, with no money to pay for accommodation or even to buy food. So it was that the area around Tripoli, which had once played such a pivotal role in slavery in the days of the Barbary corsairs, once more fell easily into the practice of trading in slaves again.

The year following the revelations from Libya, the Global Slavery Index published figures in which they claimed that a total of 9.2 million Africans were living in servitude against their will (*Quartz Africa*, 2018). This figure included many women in forced marriages which, as we remarked above, is slightly different from slavery and certainly may not be considered as being in the same class as the chattel slavery with which this book has chiefly been concerned. Nevertheless, even removing such people from the figures still leaves us with millions of slaves in present-day Africa.

Just as slavery has returned almost as a matter of course to Libya, where it was once so widespread and popular, so to with Eritrea. Eritrea was until 1991 a province of Ethiopia and was at one time a staging post for the transportation of slaves from sub-Saharan Africa to the Arab world. We looked at this traffic in a previous chapter. Slavery now, under the rule of the man who has ruled the country since independence, Isaias Afwerki, appears to have made a comeback. Under the guise of conscription, men are forced to leave their homes and work for the state for indefinite periods of time. A committee of the United Nations has accused Afwerki of systematic human rights abuses which they say might amount to crimes against humanity (*New York Times*, 2008). Under such circumstances, compulsory work for the government, undertaken against the threat of violence, may well be said to amount to slavery.

Of course, the leader of Eritrea denies that the actions of his troops amounts to slavery and it must be said that this is something of a grey area. After all, many countries do still have conscription and once called up into the army, young recruits, whether in Africa, Asia or Europe, may well be expected to undertake physically demanding and dirty jobs.

If, as seems only too likely, slavery does still linger on in some other corners of Africa, then the reason is simple. The more remote and out of the way that an area is, the more likely that activities might be undertaken in that place which would attract unfavourable attention were they to be near areas with a greater density of population and perhaps a good mobile signal. In China, concentration camps for some Muslims are established far from towns and this means that they are not the object of prying eyes. The same almost certainly applies when it comes to slavery in Africa. Every year though, the planet shrinks metaphorically, and more and more attention may be paid to what were once inaccessible locations. In a world where every inch of the planet is relentless scanned by satellites and in which the average person can summon up a photograph of anywhere he pleases by simply looking at Google Earth on a mobile telephone, it is becoming impossible to conceal anything in the long run. This lack of secrecy and ability to watch what is happening anywhere is only likely to increase in the future and it must surely be a matter of time before there is no longer any hiding place for slave caravans or markets where slaves are auctioned off. We end this book with a consideration of this idea, the future prospects for the continuation of slavery in Africa.

Endword – The Future of Slavery in Africa

Slavery in Africa, in the sense of the chattel slavery at which we have looked in this book, is on the decline. It has mostly been replaced by other forms of servitude which, although dreadful and inhumane, may not properly be called slavery. Child labour, for instance, although widespread and regrettable, cannot really be compared with the power of life and death which the owner of slaves historically exercised over the people whom they regarded as mere possessions. After all, if child labour were to be classed as slavery, as is sometimes done when statistics are being compiled, then we would have to agree that Victorian Britain was full of slave traders and slaves.

For much the same reason, we can hardly place conscripted labour in the same category as outright slavery, especially since much of this is organized by governments. It is only 60 years since National Service in Britain was abolished. This saw young men being drafted into the armed forces in peacetime and being compelled to undertake arduous physical tasks. If we do not regard this process as slavery, then it would hardly be just or fair to apply that label to similar systems, simply because they might be operating in equatorial Africa.

What we are likely to see over the course of the coming decades is the dying out of the last real slavery in Africa, which is to say the ownership of one human being by another. We looked in the last chapter at the how this situation still exists in a few corners of the continent.

As Africa becomes more technologically advanced and the means of production in the countries of the continent increases to similar levels to those found in the industrialized countries of the West, the same arguments will militate against the continuation of slavery as worked for its abolition in the British Empire 200 years ago. We read how Adam Smith, even before the dawn of the nineteenth century, had already seen the essential flaws in the system and the way in which it held back development. Those arguments, on purely economic rather than humanitarian grounds, proved persuasive in the late eighteenth and early nineteenth centuries and it is unlikely that they will prove any less convincing in Africa as the twenty-first century draws on.

The world today is very different from that which permitted chattel slavery to flourish. Even a few, brief years ago, an escaping slave might have found himself with literally nowhere to run to. Today, the planet has shrunk, so that travel to even other continents is a practical possibility for almost everybody. It is this globalization of travel which has of course led to crises such as that which currently exists on both sides of the English Channel. Refugees and asylum-seekers, many of them from sub-Saharan Africa, have somehow managed to make their way across deserts and oceans to reach Western Europe. This is a situation which only 30 years ago would have been inconceivable. Such movement of populations has been stimulated and encouraged of course by the exponential growth in electronic communications.

Let us consider the case of a slave in central Africa a century ago. Such a person would have had no real awareness of life in any other part of the world, other than perhaps what he or she was told by some passing missionary. For all that this person knew to the contrary, running away would not be at all advantageous. How could he know that slavery was not endemic throughout the entire world? Running away from his present owner might result in being captured and becoming the property of somebody who was even more cruel and might perhaps provide less food than was now the case. In short, running away from an owner would be a prospect fraught with hazard and uncertainty. Today though, in even the smallest African town there are bound to be those with access to the Internet and word circulates among the poorest inhabitant of the town about the fact that in Britain many black African people live freely and in conditions which would to a slave in the Congo be considered as luxurious. Those who are thinking of fleeing their present conditions are assured that there is at least a chance that they will be able to live vastly improved lives, if only they can find their way north across the Sahara Desert.

This knowledge alone has been sufficient to trigger a great movement of population from Africa to Europe. Unless slaves in Africa were to be physically restrained, chained up, then they have every incentive to try and escape their present conditions and seek something better. This is hardly in the interests of anybody who owns slaves. When people have nothing and no prospect of improving their lot, no matter how hard they work, then they are apt to take desperate measures to do something, anything, for a better life. If you are being paid a wage, on the other hand, and the possibility exists for furthering your own interests by remaining in one location and working hard, then this will be to everybody's advantage. It was calculations of this kind, about the long-term economic benefits to employers, which really motivated the abolition of slavery and serfdom in other parts of the world and there is no reason to suppose that those same forces will not be at work in Africa as the twenty-first century progresses.

There will doubtless be blips along the way of this progress towards a continent which is wholly free of the scourge of slavery. We looked at one such aberrant event in the last chapter, the black migrants who ended up trapped in Libya and auctioned off to the highest bidder. It is perhaps inevitable that in a continent which has never, since the earliest recorded history, been free of slavery, that the road to complete abolition will be a little bumpy.

Unless something happens to reverse the process, Africa, like the rest of the developing world, is likely to change dramatically over the coming decades. Just as in the nations of South and East Asia, African countries too will become more prosperous and advanced, at least in terms of material possessions and measured by the standard of living. There were, within living memory, conditions of servitude in the Indian subcontinent which were all but indistinguishable from slavery. As these countries have grown more similar in an industrial and technological sense to Western nations, practices which might be mistaken for slavery have, as a matter of course, tended to melt away. It is probably inevitable that this will also happen in Africa. We remember how the end of slavery in Egypt came about not just through the interference of the British, but more importantly because educated Egyptians knew that the institution had no place in a modern society. Something of this same realization will surely come to all parts of Africa in the coming decades. At the moment, Africa is the world's last bastion of naked and unashamed chattel slavery, but with every passing year the practice declines. It is all but unthinkable that by the end of this century there will be a single real slave left on the entire continent.

We have in this book examined the history of Africa from roughly 2500 BC up to the present day and found that there has never been any time over the course of those 4,500 years when slavery was not being practised somewhere on the continent. This period of time is roughly ten times greater than the centuries during which the transatlantic slave trade was taking place. It has already been observed that it is this relatively short span of time though which preoccupies modern minds and can, in a sense, be said to define slavery, at least as far as the average person in the West is concerned.

Once we view the world from a broader perspective, both temporally and spatially, it becomes obvious that the transatlantic trade was no special case, either in the sense that it was a slave trade, nor in the numbers of victims or the cruelty of the conditions under which they were transported and compelled to work. Taking this wide view of the history of humanity causes us to find the idea of widespread slavery in Africa, practised by Africans themselves, less surprising than it might be when the concept is first encountered. When we observe that every ancient society, with few exceptions, which reached a certain level of sophistication then begins to be stratified into a hierarchy, with a king or priest at the top and slaves making up the lowest level, we simply ask ourselves why Africa should have been any different from this general rule? The answer to this question was posed and answered in the Introduction and it amounts to a type of racial prejudice. We have at the back of our minds the bizarre idea that people whose skins are black and brown are somehow more natural and good than white people in Europe or the United States. They and their ancestors were, in some mysterious way, more disposed to be kind to each other. This distorted view of history is explicitly advanced today as a serious thesis by certain academics in the United States. We learned in the Introduction of Professor Brittney Cooper, of Rutgers University in the United States, who seemingly believes that slavery and colonialism are both inventions of white people and that left to their own devices, black people and brown would not have dreamed of enslaving each other. In the Introduction, we also discussed the idea of the 'noble savage' and this is really just another manifestation of that same, quaint fiction.

There has been, in the wake of the Black Lives Matter protests which erupted in the summer of 2020, a tendency to assume that all the evils and ills which have blighted human history have their origins in the actions of white people. Slavery is explicitly included in this catalogue of undesirable practices, which exculpates black people from any voluntary involvement in such a ghastly business. It is to be hoped that this book has demolished this naive belief and shown readers that slavery was no less common in Africa than it was in any other of the continents.

Bibliography

Allen, Gardner (1905), *Our Navy and the Barbary Corsairs*, Boston: Houghton Mifflin.

Andrewes, Antony (1971), *Greek Society*, London: Pelican Books.

Apley, Alice (2000), *Igbo-Ukwu (ca. 9th Century)*, *Heilbrunn Timeline of Art History*, New York: The Metropolitan Museum of Art.

Baker, Samuel White (1867), *The Nile Tributaries Of Abyssinia; And The Sword Of Hamran Arabs*, London: Macmillan.

Barbot, Jean (1999), *Barbot on Guinea: Volumes I & II: The Writings of Jean Barbot on West Africa*, London: Hakluyt Society.

Barker, A.J. (1971), *The Rape of Ethiopia 1936*, New York: Ballantine Books.

Bernal, Martin (1987), *Black Athena: The Afroasiatic Roots of Classical Civilization*, New Brunswick NJ: Rutgers University Press.

BBC (2017), *Libya migrant 'slave market' footage sparks outrage*, 18 November 2021.

Boyd, Julian P.; Bryan, Mina; and Hutter, Elizabeth L. (eds) (1953), *The Papers of Thomas Jefferson*, Princeton: Princeton University Press.

Bradley, K.; and Cartledge, P. (eds) (2011), *The Cambridge World History of Slavery*, Cambridge: Cambridge University Press.

Brewster, Paul G. (1971), 'The Foundation Sacrifice Motif in Legend, Folksong, Game, and Dance', *Zeitschrift Für Ethnologie* 96, no. 1 (1971), 71–89.

Bridge, Anthony (1988), *Suleiman the Magnificent: Scourge of Heaven*, New York: Hippocrene Books.

Briggs, Asa (1983), *A Social History of England*, New York: The Viking Press.

Brown, Michael J. (1970), *Itinerant Ambassador: The Life of Sir Thomas Roe*, Lexington: University Press of Kentucky.

Casson, Lionel (1989), *The Periplus Maris Erythraei: Text With Introduction, Translation, and Commentary*, Princeton: Princeton University Press.

Chami, Felix A. (2002), *The Graeco-Romans and Paanchea/Azania: Sailing in the Erythraean Sea; Red Sea Trade and Travel*, London: The British Museum.

Coe, Michael D. and Houston, Stephen (2015), *The Maya*, London: Thames & Hudson.

Cooper, Brittney (2021), *Unpacking The Attacks on Critical Race Theory*, The Root YouTube channel, 21 September 2021.

Cooper, Keith (2019), *The Contact Paradox*, London: Bloomsbury Publishing.

Cotterell, Arthur (ed.) (1980), *The Penguin Encyclopaedia of Ancient Civilizations*, New York: Mayflower Books.

Coupland, Reginald (1938), *East Africa and its Invaders. From the Earliest Times to the Death of Seyyid Said in 1856*, Oxford: Clarendon Press.

Crawford, Steve (2010), *Strange But True Military Facts*, Barnsley: Pen & Sword Books.

Cunliffe, Barry (2001), *The Penguin Atlas of British and Irish History*, London: Penguin Books.

Curtin, Philip D. (1999), *The Rise and Fall of the Plantation Complex*, Cambridge: Cambridge University Press.

Daily Telegraph (2017), 'Memory of Cornish coast dwellers kidnapped for slavery "culturally erased" ', 30 December 2017.

Dalby, Andrew (1998), *Dictionary of Languages*, London: Bloomsbury Publishing.

Dalrymple, William (2004), *White Mughals: Love and Betrayal in Eighteenth-century India*, London: Harper Perennial.

D'Arms, John H. and Kopf, E. Christian (1980), *Seaborne Commerce of Ancient Rome: Studies in Archaeology and History*, Rome: American Academy in Rome.

Davison, Michael Worth (ed.) (1992), *Everyday Life Through the Ages*, London: Readers' Digest Association.

Defrémery, C. and Sanguinetti, B.R. (eds) (1858), *Voyages d'Ibn Batoutah* (Volume 4) (in French and Arabic), Paris: Société Asiatic.

Desanges, J. (1990), *General History of Africa, vol. II: Ancient Civilizations of Africa*, UNESCO.

Drummond, Henry (1889), *Tropical Africa*, London: Hodder and Stoughton.

Eliot, Sir Charles (1905), *The East Africa Protectorate*, London: Edward Arnold.

Elleman, Bruce, Rosenberg, David and Forbes, Andrew (2010), *Piracy and Maritime Crime: Historical and Modern Case Studies*, Newport (US): Naval War College Press.

Epstein, Isidore (1959), *Judaism*, London: Penguin Books.

Equiano, Olaudah (1789), *The Interesting Narrative of the Life of Olaudah Equiano or Gustavus Vassa, the African*, London: Middlesex Hospital.

Everett, Suzanne (1997), *History of Slavery*, London: Grange Books.

Falkus, Christopher (1994), *Life in the Age of Exploration*, London: Readers' Digest Association.

Finkelman, P. and Miller, J.C. (eds), (1998), *MacMillan Encyclopedia of World Slavery*, New York: MacMillan.

Fleisher, Jeffrey; Lane, Paul; LaViolette, Adria; Horton, Mark; Pollard, Edward; Quintana Morales, Eréndira; Vernet, Thomas; Christie, Annalisa; and Wynne-Jones, Stephanie (2015), 'When Did the Swahili Become Maritime?', *American Anthropologist*, 2015 Mar; 117(1), 100–15.

Foulke, William Dudley (trans.) (1974), *History of the Lombards*, Philadelphia: Philadelphia University Press.

Fremont-Barnes, Gregory (2006), *The Wars of the Barbary Pirates*, London: Osprey.

Gearon, Eamonn (2011), *The Sahara: A Cultural History*, Oxford: Signal Books.

Gilbert, Martin (1998), *Descent into Barbarism: A History of the Twentieth Century 1933 – 1951*, London: HarperCollins.

Grant, Reg (2009), *Slavery*, London: Dorling Kindersley.

Greengrass, Mark (2014), *Christendom Destroyed: Europe 1517 – 1648*, London: Penguin.

Guardian (2006), '46 million people living as slaves, latest global index reveals', 1 June 2016.

Guardian (2021), 'Levelling up Pompeii: grave shows how a former slave went far', 21 August 2021.

Guardian (2021), 'Shackled skeleton identified as rare evidence of slavery in Roman Britain', 7 June 2021.

Hallett, Robin (1974), *Africa since 1875: A Modern History*, Ann Arbor: The University of Michigan Press.

Harris, David (2012), *Civil War and Democracy in West Africa: Conflict Resolution, Elections and Justice in Sierra Leone and Liberia*, London: Bloomsbury Academic.

Hawkes, Jacquetta (1973), *The First Great Civilizations*, London: Hutchinson.

Hellie, Richard (1993), *Slavery, The New Encyclopaedia Britannica, XXVII, 288-300*, Chicago: Encyclopaedia Britannica Inc.

Herodotus (2003), *The Histories*, London: Penguin Books.

Hibbert, Christopher (ed.) (1970), *The Pen and the Sword*, London: George Weidenfeld & Nicolson.

Holroyd, John, Earl of Sheffield (1783), *Observations on the commerce of the American States with Europe and the West Indies: including the several articles of import and export, and on the tendency of a bill now depending in Parliament*, London: J. Debrett.

Homer, trans. Martin Hammond (1987), *The Iliad*, London: Penguin Classics.

Hreinsson, Karl Smari and Nichols, Adam (trans.) (2016), *The Travels of Reverend Olafur Egilsson (Reisubok Sera Olafs Egilssonar): The Story of the Barbary corsair raid on Iceland in 1627*, Washington: Catholic University of America Press.

Jayasuriya, S. and Pankhurst, Richard (2003), *The African Diaspora in the Indian Ocean*, Trenton NJ: Africa World Press.

Keys, David (2004), 'Kingdom of the Sands', *Archaeology*, Vol. 57 No. 2, March/April 2004.

Kipling, Rudyard and Fletcher, C.R.L. (1911), *A School History of England*, Oxford: Clarendon Press.

Law, R.C.C. (1967), *The Journal of African History* Vol. 8, No. 2 (1967), Cambridge: Cambridge University Press, pp. 181–200.

Levtzion, Nehemia and Hopkins, John F.P. (eds) (2000), *Corpus of Early Arabic Sources for West Africa*, New York: Marcus Weiner Press.

Lewis, John E. (ed.) (1998), *The Mammoth Book of How it Happened*, London: Robinson Publishing.

Loprieno, Antonio (2012), *Encyclopedia of Egyptology*, UCLA.

MacDonald, George F. (1996), *Haida: Children of the Eagle*, Gatineau: Canadian Museum of History.

Mallory, J.P (1989), *In Search of the Indo-Europeans*, London: Thames and Hudson.

Martin, Peter J. (1991), 'The Zanzibar Clove Industry', *Economic Botany* Vol. 45, No. 4 (Oct–Dec. 1991), New York: Springer.

Mattingly, David (ed.), (2003), *Archaeology of Fazzan. Volume 1*, London: Society for Libyan Studies.

Meredith, Martin (2014), *The Fortunes of Africa*, New York: PublicAffairs.

Meynard, Charles Barbier de (trans.) (1865), *Des routes et des Provinces*, Paris: Journal Asiatique.

Miers, Suzanne and Kopytoff, Igor (1977), *Slavery in Africa: Historical and Anthropological Perspectives*, Madison: University of Wisconsin Press.

Milkias, Paulos; and Metaferia, Getachew (2005), *The Battle of Adwa: Reflections on Ethiopia's Historic Victory against European Colonialism*, New York: Algora Publishing.

Miller, J. Innes (1969), *The Cinnamon Route; The Spice Trade of The Roman Empire: 29 B.C. to A.D. 641*, Oxford: Oxford University Press.

Milton, Giles (2005), *White Gold: The Extraordinary Story of Thomas Pellow and North Africa's One Million European Slaves*, London: John Murray.

Moore-Harell, Alice (1999), 'Economic and political aspects of the slave trade in Ethiopia and the Sudan in the second half of the nineteenth century', *International Journal of African Historical Studies*, 32, 2-3, 407–21.

National Geographic (2010), 'Underground "Fossil Water" Running Out', Brian Handwerk, 8 May 2010.

N'Diaye, Tidiane (2008), *Le Génocide Voilé: Enquête historique*, Paris: Gallimard.

New York Times (2008), 'Torture and Other Rights Abuses are Widespread in Eritrea, U.N. Panels Says', 8 June 2008.

Noel-Buxton, Lord (1932), 'Slavery in Abyssinia', *International Affairs* (Royal Institute of International Affairs 1931-1939), Vol. 11, No. 4 (Jul., 1932), Oxford: Oxford University Press.

Northup, Solomon (1853), *Twelve Years a Slave*, Auburn: Derby and Miller.

O Domhnaill, Ronan Gearoid (2015), *Fado Fado: More Tales of Lesser-Known Irish History*, London: Matador.

Oliver, Roland (1977), *The Cambridge History of Africa, Volume 3: From c.1050 to c.1600*, Cambridge: Cambridge University Press.

Oluwatayo-Adeuyan, Jacob (2011), *The Return of the Tidal Flow of the Middle Passage*, Bloomington: AuthorHouse.

Ó Súilleabháin, Seán (1945), 'Foundation Sacrifices', *The Journal of the Royal Society of Antiquaries of Ireland* Vol. 75, No. 1 (Mar. 1945).

Pandya, Yatin and Rawal, Trupti (2002), *The Ahmedabad chronicle, imprints of a millennium*, Ahmedabad: Vastu Shilpa Foundation for Studies and Research in Environmental Design.

Pankhurst, Richard (1968), *Economic History of Ethiopia, 1800–1935*, Addis Ababa.

Parkinson, C. Northcote (1977), *Britannia Rules: The Classic Age of Naval History 1793–1815*, London: Weidenfeld and Nicolson.

Peach, L. du Garde (1960), *David Livingstone*, Loughborough, Wills & Hepworth.

Pelteret, David A.E. (2001), *Slavery in Early Medieval England from the Reign of Alfred Until the twelfth century (Studies in Anglo-Saxon History)*, Martlesham: Boydell Press.

Penzer, N.M. (2005), *The Harem: Inside the Grand Seraglio of the Turkish Sultans*, New York: Dover Publications.

Pepys, Samuel (1661), *The Diary of Samuel Pepys: Volume I 1660*, 2001 edition, New York: Random House.

Pipes, Daniel (1981), *Slave Soldiers and Islam: The Genesis of a Military System*, New Haven: Yale University Press.

Plato, trans. H.D.P. Lee (2007), *The Republic*, London: Penguin Books.

Pope-Hennessy, James (1967), *The Sins of the Fathers*, London: Weidenfeld & Nicolson.

Prowse, Tracy L.; Schwarcz, Henry P.; Garnsey, Peter; Knyf, Martin; Macchiarelli, Roberto; and Bondiolo, Luca (2007), 'Isotopic Evidence for age-related Immigration to Imperial Rome', *American Journal of Physical Anthropology*, 132 (4), 510–19.

Quartz Africa (2018), 'Africa is again the world's epicenter of modern-day slavery', 23 July 2018.

Regan, Geoffrey (1993), *More Military Blunders*, London: Guinness Publishing.

Reilly, Sir Bernard (1960), *Aden and the Yemen*, London: Her Majesty's Stationery Office.

Reuters (2010), 'Egypt tombs suggest pyramids not built by slaves', 10 January 2010.

Robinson, Andrew (2002), *Lost Languages*, Bath: The Bath Press.

Rodgers, N. (2007), *Ireland, Slavery and Anti-Slavery: 1612 – 1865*, London: Palgrave Macmillan.

Rodriguez, Junius P. (1997), *The Historical Encyclopaedia of World Slavery*, Santa Barbara: ABC-CLIO.

Roland, Paul (2012), *The Nuremberg Trials*, London: Arcturus Publishing.

Saco, Jose Antonio (1879), *HISTORIA DE LA ESCLAVITUD DE LA RAZA AFRICANA EN EL NUEVO IIJNIIO*, Barcelona: Imprenta de Jaime Jepus.

Schoff, Wilfred Harvey (ed.) (1912), *The Periplus of the Erythraean Sea: Travel and Trade in the Indian Ocean by a Merchant of the First Century*, New York: Longmans, Green.

Schuenemann, Verena J.; Peltzer, Alexander; Welte, Beatrix; Pelt, W. Paul van; Molak, Martyna; Chuan-Chao Wang, Furtwängler, Anja; Urban, Christian; Reiter, Ella; Nieselt, Kay; Teßmann, Barbara; Francken, Michael; Harvati, Katerina; Haak, Wolfgang; Schiffels, Stephan; and Krause, Johannes (2017), *Ancient Egyptian mummy genomes suggest an increase of Sub-Saharan African ancestry in post-Roman periods*, London: Nature Communications.

Seaver, George (1957), *David Livingstone, His Life and Letters*, London: Lutterworth Press.

Seldes, George (1935), *World Panorama, 1918 – 1935*, New York: Blue Ribbon Books.

Shah, Anish M.; Tamang, Rakesh; Moorjani, Priya; Rani, Deepa Selvi; Govindaraj, Periyaasamy; Kulkarni, Gururaj; Bhattacharya, Tanmoy; Mustak, Mohammed S.; Bhaskar L.V.K.S.; Reddy, Alla G.; Gadhvi, Dharmendra; Gai, Parmod B.; Chaubey, Gyaneshwer; Nick Patterson, Nick; Reich, David; Tyler-Smith, Chris; Singh, Lalji; and Thangaraj, Kumarasamy (2011), 'Indian Siddis; African Descendants with Indian Admixture', *American Journal of Human Genetics*, 2011 Jul 15; 89(1), 154–61.

Shaw, Thurston (1970), *Igbo-Ukwe*, Evanson Il: Northwestern University Press.

Singh, Upinder (2009), *A History of Ancient and early Medieval India: From the Stone Age to the 12th Century*, Harlow: Pearson Education.

Smith, Abdullahi (1972), *History of West Africa*, New York: Columbia University Press.

Smith, Adam (1776), *An Inquiry into the Nature and Causes of the Wealth of Nations*, London: W. Strahan and T. Cadell.

Snodgrass, Marry Ellen (2004), *Encyclopaedia of Kitchen History*, London: Routledge.

Sowada, Karin (2018), *Did Slaves Build the Pyramids?*, Sydney: Macquarie University.

Strabo (1923), *Geography*, translated by Horace Leonard Jones and published by the Loeb Classical Library.

Swanson, Claude A. (ed.) (1939), *Naval Documents Related to the United States Wars with the Barbary Powers*, Washington D.C.: U.S. Government Printing Office

Syed, Muzaffar Husein (2011), *A Concise History of Islam*, India: VIJ Books (India), Pty.

Taylor, Stephen (2012), *Commander: The Life and Exploits of Britain's Greatest Frigate Captain*, London: Faber and Faber.

Thorlby, Anthony (ed.), (1969), *The Penguin Companion to Literature: European*, London: Penguin Books.

Tracy, Larissa (ed.), (2013), *Castration and Culture in the Middle Ages*, Martlesham: D.S. Brewer.

Trevelyan, G.M. (1942), *History of England*, New York: Longmans Green.

Trigger, Bruce G. (2003), *Understanding Early Civilizations: A Comparative Study*, New York: Cambridge University Press.

Webb, Simon (2020), *The Forgotten Slave Trade: The White European Slaves of Islam*, Barnsley: Pen & Sword Books.

Wharton, Francis (compiler) (1888), *The Revolutionary Diplomatic Correspondence of the United States*, Washington.

Williams, Brenda (2006), *Ancient Britain*, Andover: Jarrold Publishing.

Williams, Eric (1970), *From Columbus to Castro: The History of the Caribbean from 1492 – 1969*, London: Andre Deutsch.

Wilson, Jean and Roerhrborn, Claus (1999), 'Long-Term Consequences of Castration in Men: Lessons from the Skopzy and the Eunuchs of the Chinese and Ottoman Courts', *The Journal of Clinical Endocrinology & Metabolism*, Vol. 84, Issue 12, 1 December 1999, pp. 4324–31.

Yemitan, Oladipo (1987), *Madame Tinubu: Merchant and King-maker*, Lagos: University Press.

Ziegler, Philip (1990), *Omdurman*, Barnsley: Pen and Sword Books.

Index